Marx Machiavelli Chesterton Emerson Joyce Abbott Hardy Montaigne Cooper Austen Defoe Melville Haggard Hugo Eliot Grimm Christie Carroll Stoker Molière Wilde Maupassant Byron Schiller Engels Fitzgerald Einstein Garnett Hawthorne Smith Kafka Goethe Dostoyevsky Hall Cotton Baum Kipling Doyle Willis Leslie Dumas Henry Nietzsche Flaubert Turgenev Balzac Stockton Vatsyayana Crane Burroughs Verne Whitman Gogol Curtis Tocqueville Vinci Homer Widger Tolstoy Busch Darwin Thoreau Potter Freud Zola Twain Plato Scott Lawrence Kant Jowett Stevenson Dickens Andersen Burton Hesse Harte Cervantes London Descartes Poe Aristotle Wells Voltaire Hale James Hastings Cooke Bunner Shakespeare Richter Chambers Irving Doré Chekhov da Benedict Alcott Swift Dante Shaw Wodehouse Pushkin Newton tredition®

tredition was established in 2006 by Sandra Latusseck and Soenke Schulz. Based in Hamburg, Germany, tredition offers publishing solutions to authors and publishing houses, combined with worldwide distribution of printed and digital book content. tredition is uniquely positioned to enable authors and publishing houses to create books on their own terms and without conventional manufacturing risks.

For more information please visit: www.tredition.com

TREDITION CLASSICS

This book is part of the TREDITION CLASSICS series. The creators of this series are united by passion for literature and driven by the intention of making all public domain books available in printed format again - worldwide. Most TREDITION CLASSICS titles have been out of print and off the bookstore shelves for decades. At tredition we believe that a great book never goes out of style and that its value is eternal. Several mostly non-profit literature projects provide content to tredition. To support their good work, tredition donates a portion of the proceeds from each sold copy. As a reader of a TREDITION CLASSICS book, you support our mission to save many of the amazing works of world literature from oblivion. See all available books at www.tredition.com.

Project Gutenberg

The content for this book has been graciously provided by Project Gutenberg. Project Gutenberg is a non-profit organization founded by Michael Hart in 1971 at the University of Illinois. The mission of Project Gutenberg is simple: To encourage the creation and distribution of eBooks. Project Gutenberg is the first and largest collection of public domain eBooks.

Voyages of Samuel De Champlain —Volume 03

Samuel de Champlain

Imprint

This book is part of TREDITION CLASSICS

Author: Samuel de Champlain
Cover design: Buchgut, Berlin – Germany

Publisher: tredition GmbH, Hamburg - Germany
ISBN: 978-3-8424-6475-9

www.tredition.com
www.tredition.de

PREFACE

The present volume completes the work proposed by the Prince Society of a translation into English of the VOYAGES OF CHAMPLAIN. It includes the journals issued in 1604, 1613, and 1619, and covers fifteen years of his residence and explorations in New France.

At a later period, in 1632, Champlain published, in a single volume, an abridgment of the issues above mentioned, containing likewise a continuation of his journal down to 1631. This continuation covers thirteen additional years. But it is to be observed that the events recorded in the journal of these later years are immediately connected with the progress and local interests of the French colony at Quebec. This last work of the great explorer is of primary importance and value as constituting original material for the early history of Canada, and a translation of it into English would doubtless be highly appreciated by the local historian. A complete narrative of these events, however, together with a large amount amount of interesting matter relating to the career of Champlain derived from other sources, is given in the Memoir contained in the first volume of this work.

This English translation contains not only the complete narratives of all the personal explorations made by Champlain into the then unbroken forests of America, but the whole of his minute, ample, and invaluable descriptions of the character and habits, mental, moral, and physical of the various savage tribes with which he came in contact. It will furnish, therefore, to the student of history and the student of ethnology most valuable information, unsurpassed in richness and extent, and which cannot be obtained from any other source. To aid one or both of these two classes in their investigations, the work was undertaken and has now been completed.

E. F. S.

BOSTON, 91 BOYLSTON STREET,
April 5, 1882.

TABLE OF CONTENTS.

ILLUSTRATIONS.

THE VOYAGES

OF SIEUR DE CHAMPLAIN,

Of Saintonge, Captain in ordinary to the
King in the Marine;

OR,

A MOST FAITHFUL JOURNAL OF OBSERVATIONS made in the, exploration of New France, describing not only the countries, coasts, rivers, ports, and harbors, with their latitudes, and the various deflections of the Magnetic Needle, but likewise the religious belief of the inhabitants, their superstitions, mode of life and warfare; furnished with numerous illustrations.

Together with two geographical maps: the first for the purposes of navigation, adapted to the compass as used by mariners, which, deflects to the north-east; the other in its true meridian, with longitudes and latitudes, to which is added the Voyage to the Strait north of Labrador, from the 53d to the 63d degree of latitude, discovered in 1612 by the English when they were searching for a northerly course to China.

PARIS.

JEAN BERJON, Rue St Jean de Beauvais, at the Flying Horse, and at his store in the Palace, at the gallery of the Prisoners.

M. DC. XIII.

WITH AUTHORITY OF THE KING.

CHAPTER I.

DEPARTURE FROM FRANCE TO RETURN TO NEW FRANCE.—THE DANGERS AND OTHER EVENTS WHICH OCCURRED UP TO THE TIME OF ARRIVAL AT THE SETTLEMENT.

We set out from Honfleur on the first day of March. The wind was favorable until the eighth, when we were opposed by a wind south-southwest and west-northwest, driving us as far as latitude 42°, without our being able to make a southing, so as to sail straight forward on our course. Accordingly after encountering several heavy winds, and being kept back by bad weather, we nevertheless, through great difficulty and hardship, and by sailing on different tacks, succeeded in arriving within eighty leagues of the Grand Bank, where the fresh fishery is carried on. Here we encountered ice thirty or forty fathoms high, or more, which led us to consider what course we ought to take, fearing that we might fall in with more during the night, or that the wind changing would drive us on to it. We also concluded that this would not be the last, since we had set out from France too early in the season. We sailed accordingly during that day with short sail, as near the wind as we could. When night came, the fog arose so thick and obscure that we could scarcely see the ship's length. About eleven o'clock at night, more ice was seen, which alarmed us. But through the energy of the sailors we avoided it. Supposing that we had passed all danger, we met with still more ice, which the sailors saw ahead of our vessel, but not until we were almost upon it. When all had committed themselves to God, having given up all hope of avoiding collision with this ice, which was already under our bowsprit, they cried to the helmsman to bear off; and this ice which was very extensive drove in such a manner that it passed by without striking our vessel, which stopped short, and remained as still as if it had never moved, to let it pass. Although the danger was over, our blood was not so quickly cooled, so great had been our fear, and we praised God for delivering us from so imminent a peril. This experience being over, we passed the same night two or three other masses of ice, not less dangerous than the former ones. There was at the same time a dripping fog, and it was so cold that we could scarcely get warm. The next day we met several other large and very high masses of ice, which, in the distance, looked like islands. We, however, avoided them all, and reached the Grand Bank, where we were detained by bad weather for the space of six days. The wind growing a little milder, and very favorable, we left the banks in latitude 44° 30', which was the farthest south we could go. After sailing some sixty leagues west-northwest, we saw a vessel coming down to make us out, but which afterwards wore off to the east-northeast, to avoid a large bank of ice, which covered the entire extent of our line of vision. Concluding that there was a passage through the middle of this great floe, which was divided into two parts, we entered, in pursuance of our course, between the two, and sailed some ten leagues without seeing anything, contrary to our conjecture of a fine passage through, until evening, when we found the floe closed up. This gave us much anxiety as to what was to be done, the night being at hand and there being no moon, which deprived us of all means of returning to the point whence we had come. Yet, after due deliberation, it was resolved to try to find again the entrance by which we had come, which we set about accomplishing. But the night coming on with fog, rain, snow, and a wind so violent that we could scarcely carry our mainsail, every trace of our way was lost. For, as we were expecting to avoid the ice so as to pass out, the wind had already closed up the passage, so that we were obliged to return to the other tack. We were unable to remain longer than a quarter of an hour on one tack before taking another, in order to avoid the numerous masses of ice drifting about on all sides. We thought more than twenty times that we should never escape with our lives. The entire night was spent amid difficulties and hardships. Never was the watch better kept, for nobody wished to rest, but to strive to escape from the ice and danger. The cold was so great, that all the ropes of the vessel were so frozen and covered with large icicles that the men could not work her nor stick to the deck. Thus we ran, on this tack and that, awaiting with hope the daylight. But when it came, attended by a fog, and we saw that our labor and hardship could not avail us anything, we determined to go to a mass of ice, where we should be sheltered from the violent wind which was blowing; to haul everything down, and allow ourselves to be driven along with the ice, so that when at some distance from the rest of the ice we could make sail again, and go back to the above-mentioned bank and manage as before, until the fog should pass away, when we might go out as quickly as possible. Thus we continued the entire day until the morning of the next day, when we set sail, now on this tack now on that, finding ourselves everywhere enclosed amid large floes of ice, as if in lakes on the mainland. At evening we sighted a vessel on the other side of one of these banks of ice, which, I am sure, was in no less anxiety than ourselves. Thus we remained four or five days, exposed to these risks and extreme hardships, until one morning on looking out in all directions, although we could see no opening, yet in one place it seemed as if the ice was not thick, and that we could easily pass through. We got under weigh, and passed by a large number of *bourguignons*; that is, pieces of ice separated from the large banks by the violence of the winds. Having reached this bank of ice, the sailors proceeded to provide themselves with large oars and pieces of wood, in order to keep off the blocks of ice we met. In this way we passed this bank, but not without touching some pieces of ice, which did no good to our vessel, although they inflicted no essential damage. Being outside, we praised God for our deliverance. Continuing our course on the next day, we encountered other pieces, in which we became so involved that we found ourselves surrounded on all sides, except where we had entered. It was accordingly necessary to turn back, and endeavor to double the southern point. This we did not succeed in doing until the second day, passing by several small pieces of ice, which had been separated from the main bank. This latter was in latitude 44° 30'. We sailed until the morning of the next day, towards the northwest, north- northwest, when we met another large ice bank, extending as far as we could see east and west. This, in the distance, seemed like land; for it was so level that it might properly be said to have been made so on purpose. It was more than eighteen feet high, extending twice as far under water. We calculated that we were only some fifteen leagues from Cape Breton, it being the 26th day of the month. These numerous encounters with ice troubled us greatly. We were also fearful that the passage between Capes Breton and Raye would be closed, and that we should be obliged to keep out to sea a long time before being able to enter. Unable to do anything else, we were obliged to run out to sea again some four or five leagues, in order to double another point of the above-mentioned grand ice bank, which continued on our west-southwest. After turning on the other tack to the northwest, in order to double this point, we sailed some seven leagues, and then steered to the north-northwest some three leagues, when we observed another ice bank. The night approached, and the fog came on so that we put to sea to pass the remainder of the night, purposing at daybreak to return and reconnoitre the last mentioned ice. On the twenty-seventh day of the month, we sighted land west-northwest of us, seeing no ice on the north- northeast. We approached nearer for the sake of a better observation, and found that it was Canseau. This led us to bear off to the north for Cape Breton Island; but we had scarcely sailed two leagues when we encountered an ice bank on the northeast. Night coming on, we were obliged to put out to sea until the next day, when we sailed northeast, and encountered more ice, bearing east, east-southeast from us, along which we coasted heading northeast and north for more than fifteen leagues. At last we were obliged to sail towards the west, greatly to our regret, inasmuch as we could find no passage, and should be obliged to withdraw and sail back on our track. Unfortunately for us we were overtaken by a calm, so that it seemed as if the swell of the sea would throw us upon the ice bank just mentioned, and we got ready to launch our little boat, to use in case of necessity. If we had taken refuge on the above-mentioned ice it would only have been to languish and die in misery. While we were deliberating whether to launch our boat, a fresh breeze arose to our great delight, and thus we escaped from the ice. After we had sailed two leagues, night came on, with a very thick fog, causing us to haul down our sail, as we could not see, and as there were several large pieces of ice in our way, which we were afraid of striking. Thus we remained the entire night until the next day, which was the twenty-ninth, when the fog increased to such an extent that we could scarcely see the length of the vessel. There was also very little wind. Yet we did not fail to set sail, in order to avoid the ice. But, although expecting to extricate ourselves, we found ourselves so involved in it that we could not tell on which side to tack. We were accordingly again compelled to lower sail, and drift until the ice should allow us to make sail. We made a hundred tacks on one side and the other, several times fearing that we were lost. The most self-possessed would have lost all judgment in such a juncture; even the greatest navigator in the world. What alarmed us still more was the short distance we could see, and the fact that the night was coming on, and that we could not make a shift of a quarter of a league without finding a bank or some ice, and a great deal of floating ice, the smallest piece of which would have been sufficient to cause the loss of any vessel whatever. Now, while we were still sailing along amid the ice, there arose so strong a wind that in a short time the fog broke away, affording us a view, and suddenly giving us a clear air and fair sun. Looking around about us, we found that we were shut up in a little lake, not so much as a league and a half in circuit. On the north we perceived the island of Cape Breton, nearly four leagues distant, and it seemed to us that the passage-way to Cape Breton was still closed. We also saw a small ice bank astern of our vessel, and the ocean beyond that, which led us to resolve to go beyond the bank, which was divided. This we succeeded in accomplishing without striking our vessel, putting out to sea for the night, and passing to the southeast of the ice. Thinking now that we could double this ice bank, we sailed east-northeast some fifteen leagues, perceiving only a little piece of ice. At night we hauled down the sail until the next day, when we perceived another ice bank to the north of us, extending as far as we could see. We had drifted to within nearly half a league of it, when we hoisted sail, continuing to coast along this ice in order to find the end of it. While sailing along, we sighted on the first day of May a vessel amid the ice, which, as well as ourselves, had found it difficult to escape from it. We backed our sails in order to await the former, which came full upon us, since we were desirous of ascertaining whether it had seen other ice. On its approach we saw that it was the son [1] of Sieur de Poutrincourt, on his way to visit his father at the settlement of Port Royal. He had left France three months before, not without much reluctance, I think, and still they were nearly a hundred and forty leagues from Port Royal, and well out of their true course. We told them we had sighted the islands of Canseau, much to their satisfaction, I think, as they had not as yet sighted any land, and were steering straight between Cape St. Lawrence and Cape Raye, in which direction they would not have found Port Royal, except by going overland. After a brief conference with each other we separated, each following his own course. The next day we sighted the islands of St. Pierre, finding no ice. Continuing our course we sighted on the following day, the third of the month, Cape Raye, also without finding ice. On the fourth we sighted the island of St. Paul, and Cape St. Lawrence, being some eight leagues north of the latter. The next day we sighted Gaspé. On the seventh we were opposed by a northwest wind, which drove us out of our course nearly thirty-five leagues, when the wind lulled, and was in our favor as far as Tadoussac, which we reached on the 13th day of May.[2] Here we discharged a cannon to notify the savages, in order to obtain news from our settlement at Quebec. The country was still almost entirely covered with snow. There came out to us some canoes, informing us that one of our pataches had been in the harbor for a month, and that three vessels had arrived eight days before. We lowered our boat and visited these savages, who were in a very miserable condition, having only a few articles to barter to satisfy their immediate wants. Besides they desired to wait until several vessels should meet, so that there might be a better market for their merchandise. Therefore they are mistaken who expect to gain an advantage by coming first, for these people are very sagacious and cunning.

On the 17th of the month I set out from Tadoussac for the great fall,[3] to meet the Algonquin savages and other tribes, who had promised the year before to go there with my man, whom I had sent to them, that I might learn from him what he might see during the winter. Those at this harbor who suspected where I was going, in accordance with the promises which I had made to the savages, as stated above, began to build several small barques, that they might follow me as soon as possible. And several, as I learned before setting out from France, had some ships and pataches fitted out in view of our voyage, hoping to return rich, as from a voyage to the Indies.

Pont Gravé remained at Tadoussac expecting, if he did nothing there, to take a patache and meet me at the fall. Between Tadoussac and Quebec our barque made much water, which obliged me to stop at Quebec and repair the leak. This was on the 21st day of May.

ENDNOTES:

1. This was Charles de Biencourt, Sieur de Saint Just. He was closely associated with his father, Sieur de Poutrincourt, in his colony at Port Royal. *Vide* Vol. I. p. 122, note 77.

2. They left Honfleur on the first day of March, and were thus seventy-four days in reaching Tadoussac. The voyage was usually made in favorable weather in thirty days.

3. The Falls of St. Louis, near Montreal, now more commonly known as the La Chine Rapids.

CHAPTER II.

LANDING AT QUEBEC TO REPAIR THE BARQUE. – DEPARTURE FROM QUEBEC FOR THE FALL, TO MEET THE SAVAGES, AND SEARCH OUT A PLACE APPROPRIATE FOR A SETTLEMENT.

On going ashore I found Sieur du Parc, who had spent the winter at the settlement. He and all his companions were very well, and had not suffered any sickness. Game, both large and small, had been abundant during the entire winter, as they told me. I found there the Indian captain, named *Batiscan*, and some Algonquins, who said they were waiting for me, being unwilling to return to Tadoussac without seeing me. I proposed to them to take one of our company to the *Trois Rivières* to explore the place, but being unable to obtain anything from them this year I put it off until the next. Still I did not fail to inform myself particularly regarding the origin of the people living there, of which they told me with exactness. I asked them for one of their canoes, which they were unwilling to part with on any terms, because of their own need of it. For I had planned to send two or three men to explore the neighborhood of the Trois Rivières, and ascertain what there was there. This, to my great regret, I was unable to accomplish, and postponed the project to the first opportunity that might present itself.

Meanwhile I urged on the repairs to our barque. When it was ready, a young man from La Rochelle, named Tresart, asked me to permit him to accompany me to the above-mentioned fall. This I refused, replying that I had special plans of my own, and that I did not wish to conduct any one to my prejudice, adding that there were other companies than mine there, and that I did not care to open up a way and serve as guide, and that he could make the voyage well enough alone and without my help.

The same day I set out from Quebec, and arrived at the great fall on the twenty-eighth of May. But I found none of the savages who had promised me to be there on this day. I entered at once a poor canoe, together with the savage I had taken to France and one of my own men. After examining the two shores, both in the woods and on the river bank, in order to find a spot favorable for the location of a settlement, and to get a place ready for building, I went some eight leagues by land along the great fall and through the woods, which are very open, as far as a lake, [4] whither our savage conducted me. Here I observed the country very carefully. But in all that I saw, I found no place more favorable than a little spot to which barques and shallops can easily ascend, with the help of a strong wind or by taking a winding course, in consequence of the strong current. But above this place, which we named *La Place Royale*, at the distance of a league from Mont Royal, there are a great many little rocks and shoals, which are very dangerous. Near Place Royale there is a little river, extending some distance into the interior, along the entire length of which there are more than sixty acres of land cleared up and like meadows, where grain can be sown and gardens made. Formerly savages tilled these lands, [5] but they abandoned them on account of their wars, in which they were constantly engaged. There is also a large number of other fine pastures, where any number of cattle can graze. There are also the various kinds of trees found in France, together with many vines, nut and plum trees, cherries, strawberries, and other kinds of good fruit. Among the rest there is a very excellent one, with a sweet taste like that of plantains, a fruit of the Indies, as white as snow, with a leaf resembling that of nettles, and which creeps up the trees and along the ground like ivy. [6] Fish are very abundant, including all the varieties we have in France, and many very good ones which we do not have. Game is also plenty, the birds being of various kinds. There are stags, hinds, does, caribous, [7] rabbits, lynxes, [8] bears, beavers, also other small animals, and all in such large numbers, that while we were at the fall we were abundantly supplied with them.

After a careful examination, we found this place one of the finest on this river. I accordingly forthwith gave orders to cut down and clear up the woods in the Place Royale, [9] so as to level it and prepare it for building. The water can easily be made to flow around it, making of it a little island, so that a habitation can be formed as one may wish.

There is a little island some twenty fathoms from Place Royale, about a hundred paces long, where a good and strong settlement might be made. There are also many meadows, containing very good and rich potter's clay, as well adapted for brick as for building purposes, and consequently a very useful article. I had a portion of it worked up, from which I made a wall four feet thick, three or four high, and ten fathoms long, to see how it would stand during the winter, when the freshets came down, although I thought the water would not reach up to it, the ground there being twelve feet above the river, which was very high. In the middle of the river there was an island about three-quarters of a league around, where a good and strong town could be built. This we named *Isle de Sainte Hélène*. [10] This river at the fall is like a lake, containing two or three islands, and bordered by fine meadows.

On the first day of June, Pont Gravé arrived at the fall, having been unable to accomplish anything at Tadoussac. A numerous company attended and followed after him to share in the booty, without the hope of which they would have been far in the rear.

Now, while awaiting the savages, I had two gardens made, one in the meadows, the other in the woods, which I had cleared up. On the 2d of June I sowed some seeds, all of which came up finely, and in a short time, attesting the good quality of the soil.

We resolved to send Savignon, our savage, together with another, to meet his countrymen, so as to hasten their arrival. They hesitated about going in our canoe, of which they were distrustful, it being a very poor one. They set out on the 5th. The next day four or five barques arrived as an escort for us, since they could do nothing at Tadoussac.

On the 7th I went to explore a little river, along which the savages sometimes go to war, and which flows into the fall of the river of the Iroquois. [11] It is very pleasant, with meadow land more than three leagues in circuit, and much arable land. It is distant a league from the great fall, and a league and a half from Place Royale.

On the 9th our savage arrived. He had gone somewhat beyond the lake, which is ten leagues long, and which I had seen before. [12] But he met no one, and they were unable to go any farther, as their canoe gave out, which obliged them to return. They reported that after passing the fall they saw an island, where there was such a quantity of herons that the air was completely filled with them. There was a young man belonging to Sieur de Monts named Louis, who was very fond of the chase. Hearing this, he wished to go and satisfy his curiosity, earnestly entreating our savage to take him to the place. To this the savage consented, taking also a captain of the Montagnais, a very respectable person, whose name was *Outetoucos*. On the following morning Louis caused the two savages to be called, and went with them in a canoe to the island of the herons. This island is in the middle of the fall. [13] Here they captured as many herons and other birds as they wanted, and embarked again in their canoe. Outetoucos, contrary to the wish of the other savage, and against his remonstrances, desired to pass through a very dangerous place, where the water fell more than three feet, saying that he had formerly gone this way, which, however, was false. He had a long discussion in opposition to our savage, who wished to take him on the south side, along the mainland, [14] where they usually go. This, however, Outetoucos did not wish, saying that there was no danger. Our savage finding him obstinate yielded to his desire. But he insisted that at least a part of the birds in the canoe should be taken out, as it was overloaded, otherwise he said it would inevitably fill and be lost. But to this he would not consent, saying that it would be time enough when they found themselves in the presence of danger. They accordingly permitted themselves to be carried along by the current. But when they reached the precipice, they wanted to throw overboard their load in order to escape. It was now, however, too late, for they were completely in the power of the rapid water, and were straightway swallowed up in the whirlpools of the fall, which turned them round a thousand times. For a long time they clung to the boat. Finally the swiftness of the water wearied them so that this poor Louis, who could not swim at all, entirely lost his presence of mind, and, the canoe going down, he was obliged to abandon it. As it returned to the surface, the two others who kept holding on to it, saw Louis no more, and thus he died a sad death. [15] The two others continued to hold on to the canoe. When, however, they were out of danger, this Outetoucos, being naked and having confidence in his swimming powers, abandoned it in the expectation of reaching the shore, although the water still ran there with great rapidity. But he was drowned, for he had been so weakened and overcome by his efforts that it was impossible for him to save himself after abandoning the canoe. Our savage Savignon, understanding himself better, held firmly to the canoe until it reached an eddy, whither the current had carried it. Here he managed so well that, notwithstanding his suffering and weariness, he approached the shore gradually, when, after throwing the water out of the canoe, he returned in great fear that they would take vengeance upon him, as the savages do among themselves, and related to us this sad story, which caused us great sorrow.

On the next day I went in another canoe to the fall, together with the savage and another member of our company, to see the place where they had met with their accident, and find, if possible, the remains. But when he showed me the spot, I was horrified at beholding such a terrible place, and astonished that the deceased should have been so lacking in judgment as to pass through such a fearful place, when they could have gone another way. For it is impossible to go along there, as there are seven or eight descents of water one after the other, the lowest three feet high, the seething and boiling of the water being fearful. A part of the fall was all white with foam, indicating the worst spot, the noise of which was like thunder, the air resounding with the echo of the cataracts. After viewing and carefully examining this place, and searching along the river bank for the dead bodies, another very light shallop having proceeded meanwhile on the other bank also, we returned without finding anything.

* * * * *

CHAMPLAIN'S EXPLANATION OF THE ACCOMPANYING MAP.

LE GRAND SAULT ST. LOUIS.

A. Small place that I had cleared up. B. Small pond. C. Small islet, where I had a stone wall made. D. Small brook, where the barques are kept. E. Meadows where the savages stay when they come to this region. F. Mountains seen in the interior. G. Small pond. H. Mont Royal. I. Small brook. L. The fall. M. Place on the north side, where the savages transfer their canoes by land. N. Spot where one of our men and a savage were drowned. O. Small rocky islet. P. Another islet where birds make their nests. Q. Heron island. R. Another island in the fall. S. Small islet T. Small round islet. V. Another islet half covered with water. X. Another islet, where there are many river birds. Y. Meadows. Z. Small river. 2. Very large and fine islands. 3. Places which are bare when the water is low, where there are great eddies, as at the main fall. 4. Meadows covered with water 5. Very shallow places. 6. Another little islet. 7. Small rocks. 8. Island St. Hélène. 9. Small island without trees. oo. Marshes connecting with the great fall.

ENDNOTES:

4. This journey of eight leagues would take them as far as the Lake of Two Mountains.

5. This little river is mentioned by Champlain in his Voyage of 1603, Vol. I. p. 268. It is represented on early maps as formed by two small streams, flowing, one from the north or northeastern, and the other from the southern side of the mountain, in the rear of the city of Montreal, which unite some distance before they reach the St. Lawrence, flowing into that river at Point Callières. These little brooks are laid down on Champlain's local map, *Le Grand Sault St. Louis*, on Charlevoix's *Carte de l'Isle de Montréal*, 1744, and on Bellin's *L'Isle de Montréal*, 1764; but they have disappeared on modern maps, and probably are either extinct or are lost in the sewerage of the city, of which they have become a part. We have called the stream formed by these two brooks, note 190, Vol. I., *Rivière St. Pierre*. On Potherie's map, the only stream coming from the interior is so named. *Vide Histoire de L'Amerique* par M. de Bacqueville de la Potherie, 1722, p. 311. On a map in Greig's *Hochelaga Depicta*, 1839, it is called St. Peter's River. The same stream on Bouchette's map, 1830, is denominated Little River. It seems not unlikely that a part of it was called, at one time, Rivière St. Pierre, and another part Petite Rivière.

It is plain that on this stream was situated the sixty acres of cleared land alluded to in the text as formerly occupied by the savages.

It will be remembered that seventy-six years anterior to this, in 1535, Jacques Cartier discovered this place, which was then the seat of a large and flourishing Indian town. It is to be regretted that Champlain did not inform us more definitely as to the history of the former occupants of the soil. Some important, and we think conclusive, reasons have been assigned for supposing that they were a tribe of the Iroquois. Among others may be mentioned the similarity in the construction of their towns and houses or cabins, the identity of their language as determined by a collation of the words found in Cartier's journal with the language of the Iroquois; and to these may be added the traditions obtained by missionaries and others, as cited by Laverdière, to which we must not, however, attach too much value. *Vide Laverdière in loco.* While it seems probable that the former occupants were of the Iroquois family, it is impossible to determine whether on retiring they joined the Five Nations in the State of New York, or merged themselves with the Hurons, who were likewise of Iroquois origin.

6. I am unable to identify this plant. Its climbing propensity and the color of its fruit suggest *Rhus radicans*, but in other respects the similarity fails.

7. *Cerfs, Daims, Cheureuls, Caribous.* Champlain employs the names of the different species of the Cerf family as used in Europe; but as our species are different, this use of names creates some confusion. There were in Canada, the moose, the caribou, the wapiti, and the common red deer. Any enumeration by the early writers must include these, under whatever names they may be described. One will be found applying a name to a given species, while another will apply the same name to quite a different species. Charlevoix mentions the orignal (moose) caribou, the hart, and the roebuck. Under the name *hart*, he probably refers to the wapiti, *elaphus Canadensis*, and *roe-buck*, to the common red deer, *Cervus Virginianus.*

Vide Charlevoix's Letters to the Dutchess of Lesdiguieres, 1763, pp. 64-69, also Vol. I. of this work, p. 265.

8. Lynxes, *Loups-seruiers*. The compound word *loup-cervier* was significant, and was applied originally to the animal of which the stag was its natural prey, *qui attaque les cerfs*. In Europe it described the lynx, a large powerful animal of the feline race, that might well venture to attack the stag. But in Canada this species is not found. What is known as the Canadian lynx, *Felis Canadensis*, is only a large species of cat, which preys upon birds and the smaller quadrupeds. Champlain probably gives it the name *loup-servier* for the want of one more appropriate. It is a little remarkable that he does not in this list mention the American wolf, *Lupus occidentalis*, so common in every part of Canada, and which he subsequently refers to as the animal especially dreaded by the deer. *Vide postea*, pp. 139, 157.

9. The site of Place Royale was on Point Callières, so named in honor of Chevalier Louis Hector de Callières Bonnevue, governor of Montreal in 1684.

10. It seems most likely that the name of this island was suggested by the marriage which Champlain had contracted with Hélène Boullé, the year before. This name had been given to several other places. *Vide* Vol. I. pp. 104, 105.

11. *Vide* Vol. I. p. 268, note 191. *Walker and Miles's Atlas*, map 186.

12. The Lake of the Two Mountains. *Vide antea*, note 4.

13. On Champlain's local map of the Falls of St. Louis, the letter Q is wanting; but the expression, *ceste isle est au milieu du faut*, in the middle of the fall, as suggested by Laverdière, indicates that the island designated by the letter R is Heron Island. *Vide postea*, R on map at p. 18.

14. *Grand Tibie*, so in the original. This is a typographical error for *grand terre*. *Vide* Champlain, 1632, Quebec ed., p. 842.

15. The death of this young man may have suggested the name which was afterward given to the fall. He was, however, it is reasonable to suppose, hardly equal in sanctity of character to the Saint Louis of the French. Hitherto it had been called *Le Grand Saut*. But

soon after this it began to be called *Grand Saut S. Louys. Vide postea,* pp. 38, 51, 59.

CHAPTER III.

TWO HUNDRED SAVAGES RETURN THE FRENCHMAN WHO HAD BEEN ENTRUSTED TO THEM, AND RECEIVE THE SAVAGE WHO HAD COME BACK FROM FRANCE.—VARIOUS INTERVIEWS ON BOTH SIDES.

On the thirteenth day of the month [16] two hundred Charioquois [17] savages, together with the captains Ochateguin, Iroquet, and Tregouaroti, brother of our savage, brought back my servant. [18] We were greatly pleased to see them. I went to meet them in a canoe with our savage. As they were approaching slowly and in order, our men prepared to salute them with a discharge of arquebuses, muskets, and small pieces. When they were near at hand, they all set to shouting together, and one of the chiefs gave orders that they should make their harangue, in which they greatly praised us, commending us as truthful, inasmuch as I had kept the promise to meet them at this fall. After they had made three more shouts, there was a discharge of musketry twice from thirteen barques or pataches that were there. This alarmed them so, that they begged me to assure them that there should be no more firing, saying that the greater part of them had never seen Christians, nor heard thunderings of that sort, and that they were afraid of its harming them, but that they were greatly pleased to see our savage in health, whom they supposed was dead, as had been reported by some Algonquins, who had heard so from the Montagnais. The savage commended the treatment I had shown him in France, and the remarkable objects he had seen, at which all wondered, and went away quietly to their cabins, expecting that on the next day I would show them the place where I wished to have them dwell. I saw also my servant, who was dressed in the costume of the savages, who commended the treatment he had received from them. He informed me of all he had seen and learned during the winter, from the savages.

The next day I showed them a spot for their cabins, in regard to which the elders and principal ones consulted very privately. After their long consultation they sent for me alone and my servant, who had learned their language very well. They told him they desired a close alliance with me, and were sorry to see here all these shallops, and that our savage had told them he did not know them at all nor their intentions, and that it was clear that they were attracted only by their desire of gain and their avarice, and that when their assistance was needed they would refuse it, and would not act as I did in offering to go with my companions to their country and assist them, of all of which I had given them proofs in the past. They praised me for the treatment I had shown our savage, which was that of a brother, and had put them under such obligations of good will to me, that they said they would endeavor to comply with anything I might desire from them, but that they feared that the other boats would do them some harm. I assured them that they would not, and that we were all under one king, whom our savage had seen, and belonged to the same nation, though matters of business were confined to individuals, and that they had no occasion to fear, but might feel as much security as if they were in their own country. After considerable conversation, they made me a present of a hundred castors. I gave them in exchange other kinds of merchandise. They told me there were more than four hundred savages of their country who had purposed to come, but had been prevented by the following representations of an Iroquois prisoner, who had belonged to me, but had escaped to his own country. He had reported, they said, that I had given him his liberty and some merchandise, and that I purposed to go to the fall with six hundred Iroquois to meet the Algonquins and kill them all, adding that the fear aroused by this intelligence had alone prevented them from coming. I replied that the prisoner in question had escaped without my leave, that our savage knew very well how he went away, and that there was no thought of abandoning their alliance, as they had heard, since I had engaged in war with them, and sent my servant to their country to foster their friendship, which was still farther confirmed by my keeping my promise to them in so faithful a manner.

They replied that, so far as they were concerned, they had never thought of this; that they were well aware that all this talk was far from the truth, and that if they had believed the contrary they would not have come, but that the others were afraid, never having seen a Frenchman except my servant. They told me also that three hundred Algonquins would come in five or six days, if we would wait for them, to unite with themselves in war against the Iroquois; that, however, they would return without doing so unless I went. I talked a great deal with them about the source of the great river and their country, and they gave me detailed information about their rivers, falls, lakes and lands, as also about the tribes living there, and what is to be found in the region. Four of them assured me that they had seen a sea at a great distance from their country, but that it was difficult to go there, not only on account of the wars, but of the intervening wilderness. They told me also that the winter before some savages had come from the direction of Florida, beyond the country of the Iroquois, who lived near our ocean, and were in alliance with these savages. In a word, they made me a very exact statement, indicating by drawings all the places where they had been, and taking pleasure in talking to me about them; and for my part I did not tire of listening to them, as they confirmed points in regard to which I had been before in doubt. After all this conversation was concluded, I told them that we would trade for the few articles they had, which was done the next day. Each one of the barques carried away its portion; we on our side had all the hardship and venture; the others, who had not troubled themselves about any explorations, had the booty, the only thing that urges them to activity, in which they employ no capital and venture nothing.

The next day, after bartering what little they had, they made a barricade about their dwelling, partly in the direction of the wood, and partly in that of our pataches; and this they said they did for their security, in order to avoid the surprises of their enemies, which we took for the truth. On the coming night, they called our savage, who was sleeping on my patache, and my servant, who went to them. After a great deal of conversation, about midnight they had me called also. Entering their cabins, I found them all seated in council. They had me sit down near them, saying that when they met for the purpose of considering a matter, it was their custom to do so at night, that they might not be diverted by anything from attention to the subject in hand; that at night one thought only of listening, while during the day the thoughts were distracted by other objects.

But in my opinion, confiding in me, they desired to tell me privately their purpose. Besides, they were afraid of the other pataches, as they subsequently gave me to understand. For they told me that they were uneasy at seeing so many Frenchmen, who were not especially united to one another, and that they had desired to see me alone; that some of them had been beaten; that they were as kindly disposed towards me as towards their own children, confiding so much in me that they would do whatever I told them to do, but that they greatly mistrusted the others; that if I returned I might take as many of their people as I wished, if it were under the guidance of a chief; and that they sent for me to assure me anew of their friendship, which would never be broken, and to express the hope that I might never be ill disposed towards them; and being aware that I had determined to visit their country, they said they would show it to me at the risk of their lives, giving me the assistance of a large number of men, who could go everywhere; and that in future we should expect such treatment from them as they had received from us.

Straightway they brought fifty castors and four strings of beads, which they value as we do gold chains, saying that I should share these with my brother, referring to Pont Gravé, we being present together; that these presents were sent by other captains, who had never seen me; that they desired to continue friends to me; that if any of the French wished to go with them, they should be greatly pleased to have them do so; and that they desired more than ever to establish a firm friendship. After much conversation with them, I proposed that inasmuch as they were desirous to have me visit their country, I would petition His Majesty to assist us to the extent of forty or fifty men, equipped with what was necessary for the journey, and that I would embark with them on condition that they would furnish us the necessary provisions for the journey, and that I would take presents for the chiefs of the country through which we should pass, when we would return to our settlement to spend the winter; that moreover, if I found their country favorable and fertile, we would make many settlements there, by which means we should have frequent intercourse with each other, living happily in the future in the fear of God, whom we would make known to them. They were well pleased with this proposition, and begged me to shake hands upon it, saying that they on their part would do all that was possible for its fulfilment; that, in regard to provisions, we should be as well supplied as they themselves, assuring me again that they would show me what I desired to see. Thereupon, I took leave of them at daybreak, thanking them for their willingness to carry out my wishes, and entreating them to continue to entertain the same feelings.

On the next day, the 17th, they said that they were going castor-hunting, and that they would all return. On the following morning they finished bartering what little they had, when they embarked in their canoes, asking us not to take any steps towards taking down their dwellings, which we promised them. Then they separated from each other, pretending to go a hunting in different directions. They left our savage with me that we might have less distrust in them. But they had appointed themselves a rendezvous above the fall, where they knew well enough that we could not go with our barques. Meanwhile, we awaited them in accordance with what they had told us.

The next day there came two savages, one Iroquet, the other the brother of our Savignon. They came to get the latter, and ask me in behalf of all their companions to go alone with my servant to where they were encamped, as they had something of importance to tell me, which they were unwilling to communicate to any Frenchmen. I promised them that I would go.

The following day I gave some trifles to Savignon, who set out much pleased, giving me to understand that he was about to live a very irksome life in comparison with that which he had led in France. He expressed much regret at separation, but I was very glad to be relieved of the care of him. The two captains told me that on the morning of the next day they would send for me, which they did. I embarked, accompanied by my servant, with those who came. Having arrived at the fall, we went some eight leagues into the woods, where they were encamped on the shore of a lake, where I had been before.[19] They were much pleased at seeing me, and began to shout after their custom. Our Indian came out to meet me, and ask me to go to the cabin of his brother, where he at once had some meat and fish put on the fire for my entertainment. While I was there, a banquet was held, to which all the leading Indians were invited. I was not forgotten, although I had already eaten sufficiently; but, in order not to violate the custom of the country, I attended. After banqueting, they went into the woods to hold their council, and meanwhile I amused myself in looking at the country round about, which is very pleasant.

Some time after they called me, in order to communicate to me what they had resolved upon. I proceeded to them accordingly with my servant. After I had seated myself by their side, they said they were very glad to see me, and to find that I had not failed to keep my word in what I had promised them; saying that they felt it an additional proof of my affection that I continued the alliance with them, and that before setting out they desired to take leave of me, as it would have been a very great disappointment to them to go away without seeing me, thinking that I would in that case have been ill disposed towards them. They said also that what had led them to say they were going a hunting, and build the barricade, was not the fear of their enemies nor the desire of hunting, but their fear of all the other pataches accompanying me, inasmuch as they had heard it said that on the night they sent for me they were all to be killed, and that I should not be able to protect them from the others who were much more numerous; so that in order to get away they made use of this ruse. But they said if there had been only our two pataches they would have stayed some days longer, and they begged that, when I returned with my companions, I would not bring any others. To this I replied that I did not bring these, but that they followed without my invitation; that in the future, however, I would come in another manner; at which explanation they were much pleased.

And now they began again to repeat what they had promised me in regard to the exploration of the country, while I promised, with the help of God, to fulfil what I had told them. They besought me again to give them a man, and I replied that if there was any one among us who was willing to go, I should be well pleased.

They told me there was a merchant, named Bouyer, commander of a patache, who had asked them to take a young man, which request, however, they had been unwilling to grant before ascertaining whether this was agreeable to me, as they did not know whether we were friends, since he had come in my company to trade with them; also that they were in no wise under any obligations to him, but that he had offered to make them large presents.

I replied that we were in no wise enemies, and that they had often seen us conversing with each other; but that in regard to traffic each did what he could, and that the above-named Bouyer was perhaps desirous of sending this young man as I had sent mine, hoping for some return in the future, which I could also lay claim to from them; that, however, they must judge towards whom they had the greatest obligations, and from whom they were to expect the most.

They said there was no comparison between the obligations in the two cases, not only in view of the help I had rendered them in their wars against their enemies, but also of the offer of my personal assistance in the future, in all of which they had found me faithful to the truth, adding that all depended on my pleasure. They said moreover that what made them speak of the matter was the presents he had offered them, and that, if this young man should go with them, it would not put them under such obligations to this Bouyer as they were under to me, and that it would have no influence upon the future, since they only took him on account of the presents from Bouyer.

I replied that it was indifferent to me whether they took him or not, and in fact that if they took him for a small consideration I should be displeased at it, but if in return for valuable presents, I should be satisfied, provided he stayed with Iroquet; which they promised me. Then there was made on both sides a final statement of our agreements. They had with them one who had three times been made prisoner by the Iroquois, but had been successful in escaping. This one resolved to go, with nine others, to war, for the sake of revenge for the cruelties his enemies had caused him to suffer. All the captains begged me to dissuade him if possible, since he was very valiant, and they were afraid that, advancing boldly towards the enemy, and supported by a small force only, he would never return. To satisfy them I endeavored to do so, and urged all the reasons I could, which, however, availed little; for he, showing me a portion of his fingers cut off, also great cuts and burns on his body, as evidences of the manner they had tortured him, said that it was impossible for him to live without killing some of his enemies and having vengeance, and that his heart told him he must set out as soon as possible, as he did, firmly resolved to behave well.

After concluding with them, I asked them to take me back in our patache. To accomplish this, they got ready eight canoes in order to pass the fall, stripping themselves naked, and directing me to go only in my shirt. For it often happens that some are lost in passing the fall. Consequently, they keep close to each other, so as to render assistance at once, if any canoe should happen to turn over. They said to me, if yours should unfortunately overturn, not knowing how to swim, you must not think of abandoning it, and must cling to the little pieces in the middle of it, for we can easily rescue you. I am sure that even the most self-possessed persons in the world, who have not seen this place nor passed it in little boats such as they have, could not do so without the greatest apprehension. But these people are so skilful in passing falls, that it is an easy matter for them. I passed with them, which I had never before done, nor any other Christian, except my above-mentioned servant. Then we reached our barques, where I lodged a large number of them, and had some conversation with the before-mentioned Bouyer in view of the fear he entertained that I should prevent his servant from going with the savages. They returned the next day with the young man, who proved expensive to his master who had expected, in my opinion, to recover the losses of his voyage, which were very considerable, like those of many others.

One of our young men also determined to go with these savages, who are Charioquois, living at a distance of some one hundred and fifty leagues from the fall. He went with the brother of Savignon, one of the captains, who promised me to show him all that could be seen. Bouyer's man went with the above-mentioned Iroquet, an Algonquin, who lives some eighty leagues from the fall. Both went off well pleased and contented.

After the departure of the savages, we awaited the three hundred others who, as had been told us, were to come, in accordance with the promise I had made them. Finding that they did not come, all the pataches determined to induce some Algonquin savages, who had come from Tadoussac, to go to meet them, in view of a reward that would be given them on their return, which was to be at the latest not over nine days from the time of their departure, so that we might know whether to expect them or not, and be able to return to Tadoussac. This they agreed to, and a canoe left with this purpose.

On the fifth of July a canoe arrived from the Algonquins, who were to come to the number of three hundred. From it we learned that the canoe which had set out from us had arrived in their country, and that their companions, wearied by their journey, were resting, and that they would soon arrive, in fulfilment of the promise they had made; that at most they would not be more than eight days behindhand, but that there would be only twenty-four canoes, as one of their captains and many of their comrades had died of a fever that had broken out among them. They also said that they had sent many to the war, which had hindered their progress. We determined to wait for them.

But finding that this period had elapsed without their arrival, Pont Gravé set out from the fall on the eleventh of the month, to arrange some matters at Tadoussac, while I stayed to await the savages.

The same day a patache arrived, bringing provisions for the numerous barques of which our party consisted. For our bread, wine, meat, and cider had given out some days before, obliging us to have recourse to fishing, the fine river water, and some radishes which grow in great abundance in the country; otherwise we should have been obliged to return. The same day an Algonquin canoe arrived, assuring us that on the next day the twenty-four canoes were to come, twelve of them prepared for war.

On the twelfth the Algonquins arrived with some little merchandise. Before trafficking they made a present to a Montagnais Indian, the son of Anadabijou, [20] who had lately died, in order to mitigate his grief at the death of his father. Shortly after they resolved to make some presents to all the captains of the pataches. They gave to each of them ten castors, saying they were very sorry they had no more, but that the war, to which most of them were going, was the reason; they begged, however, that what they offered might be accepted in good part, saying that they were all friends to us, and to me, who was seated near them, more than to all the others, who were well disposed towards them only on account of their castors, and had not always assisted them like myself, whom they had never found double-tongued like the rest.

I replied that all those whom they saw gathered together were their friends; that, in case an opportunity should present itself, they would not fail to do their duty; that we were all friends; that they should continue to be well disposed towards us; that we would make them presents in return for those they gave us; and that they should trade in peace. This they did, and carried away what they could.

The next day they brought me privately forty castors, assuring me of their friendship, and that they were very glad of the conclusion which I had reached with the savages who had gone away, and that we should make a settlement at the fall, which I assured them we would do, making them a present in return.

After everything had been arranged, they determined to go and obtain the body of Outetoucos, who was drowned at the fall, as we have before mentioned. They went to the spot where he had been buried, disinterred him and carried him to the island of St Hélène, where they performed their usual ceremony, which is to sing and dance over the grave with festivities and banquets following. I asked them why they disinterred the body. They replied that if their enemies should find the grave they would do so, and divide the body into several pieces, which they would then hang to trees in order to offend them. For this reason they said that they transferred it to a place off from the road, and in the most secret manner possible.

On the 15th there arrived fourteen canoes, the chief over which was named *Tecouehata*. Upon their arrival all the other savages took up arms and performed some circular evolutions. After going around and dancing to their satisfaction, the others who were in their canoes also began to dance, making various movements of the body. After finishing their singing, they went on shore with a small quantity of furs, and made presents similar to those of the others. These were reciprocated by some of equal value. The next day they trafficked in what little they had, and presented me personally with thirty castors, for which I made them an acknowledgment. They begged me to continue my good will to them, which I promised to do. They spoke with me very especially respecting certain explorations towards the north, which might prove advantageous; and said, in reference to them, that if any one of my company would like to go with them, they would show him what would please me, and would treat him as one of their own children. I promised to give them a young man, at which they were much pleased. When he took leave of me to go with them, I gave him a detailed memorandum of what he was to observe while with them. After they had bartered what little they had, they separated into three parties; one for the war, another for the great fall, another for a little river which flows into that of the great fall. Thus they set out on the 18th day of the month, on which day we also departed.

The same day we made the thirty leagues from this fall to the Trois Rivières. On the 19th we arrived at Quebec, which is also thirty leagues from the Trois Rivières. I induced the most of those in each boat to stay at the settlement, when I had some repairs made and some rose-bushes set out. I had also some oak wood put on board to make trial of in France, not only for marine wainscoting, but also for windows. The next day, the 20th of July, I set out. On the 23d I arrived at Tadoussac, whence I resolved to return to France, in accordance with the advice of Pont Gravé. After arranging matters relating to our settlement, according to the directions which Sieur de Monts had given me, I embarked in the vessel of Captain Tibaut, of La Rochelle, on the 11th of August. During our passage we had an abundance of fish, such as *orades*, mackerel, and *pilotes*, the latter similar to herrings, and found about certain planks covered with *pousle-pieds*, a kind of shell-fish attaching itself thereto, and growing there gradually. Sometimes the number of these little fish is so great that it is surprising to behold. We caught also some porpoises and other species of fish. The weather was favorable as far as Belle Isle, [21] where we were overtaken by fogs, which continued three or four days. The weather then becoming fair, we sighted Alvert, [22] and arrived at La Rochelle on the 16th of September, 1611.

ENDNOTES:

16. June 13th.

17. *Charioquois*. In the issue of 1632, p. 397, Champlain has *Sauuages Hurons*. It is probable that Charioquois was only a chief of the Hurons.

18. This was the young man that had been sent to pass the winter with the Indians, in exchange for the savage which had accompanied Champlain to France. *Vide antea,* Vol. II. p. 246.

19. This was doubtless on the Lake of Two Mountains.

20. Champlain's orthography is here *Aronadabigeau. Vide* Vol. I pp. 236, 291.

21. Belle Ile. An island on the coast of Brittany in France.

22. Alvert, a village near Marennes, which they sighted as they approached La Rochelle.

CHAPTER IV.

ARRIVAL AT LA ROCHELLE.—DISSOLUTION OF THE PARTNERSHIP BETWEEN SIEUR DE MONTS AND HIS ASSOCIATES, THE SIEURS COLIER AND LE GENDRE OF ROUEN.— JEALOUSY OF THE FRENCH IN REGARD TO THE NEW DISCOVERIES IN NEW FRANCE.

Upon my arrival at La Rochelle I proceeded to visit Sieur de Monts, at Pons [23] in Saintonge, to inform him of all that had occurred during the expedition, and of the promise which the Ochateguins[24] and Algonquins had made me, on condition that we would assist them in their wars, as I had agreed. Sieur de Monts, after listening to it all, determined to go to the Court to arrange the matter. I started before him to go there also. But on the way I was unfortunately detained by the falling of a horse upon me, which came near killing me. This fall detained me some time; but as soon as I had sufficiently recovered from its effects I set out again to complete my journey and meet Sieur de Monts at Fontainebleau, who, upon his return to Paris, had a conference with his associates. The latter were unwilling to continue in the association, as there was no commission forbidding any others from going to the new discoveries and trading with the inhabitants of the country. Sieur de Monts, seeing this, bargained with them for what remained at the settlement at Quebec, in consideration of a sum of money which he gave them for their share. He sent also some men to take care of the settlement, in the expectation of obtaining a commission from His Majesty. But while he was engaged in the pursuit of this object some important matters demanded his attention, so that he was obliged to abandon it, and he left me the duty of taking the necessary steps for it. As I was about arranging the matter, the vessels arrived from New France with men from our settlement, those whom I had sent into the interior with the savages. They brought me very important information, saying that more than two hundred savages had come, expecting to find me at the great fall of St. Louis, where I had appointed a rendezvous, with the intention of assisting them according to their request. But, finding that I had not kept my promise, they were greatly displeased. Our men, however, made some apologies, which were accepted, and assured them that they would not fail to come the following year or never. The savages agreed to this on their part. But several others left the old trading-station of Tadoussac, and came to the fall with many small barques to see if they could engage in traffic with these people, whom they assured that I was dead, although our men stoutly declared the contrary. This shows how jealousy against meritorious objects gets possession of bad natures; and all they want is that men should expose themselves to a thousand dangers, to discover peoples and territories, that they themselves may have the profit and others the hardship. It is not reasonable that one should capture the lamb and another go off with the fleece. If they had been willing to participate in our discoveries, use their means, and risk their persons, they would have given evidence of their honor and nobleness, but on the contrary they show clearly that they are impelled by pure malice that they may enjoy the fruit of our labors equally with ourselves.

On this subject, and to show how many persons strive to pervert praiseworthy enterprises, I will instance again the people of St. Malo and others, who say that the profit of these discoveries belongs to them, since Jacques Cartier, who first visited Canada and the islands of New Foundland, was from their city, as if that city had contributed to the expenses of these discoveries of Jacques Cartier, who went there by the order and at the expense of King Francis I, in the years 1534 and 1535 to discover these territories now called New France. If then Cartier made any discovery at the expense of His Majesty, all his subjects have the same rights and liberties in them as the people of St. Malo, who cannot prevent others who make farther discoveries at their own expense, as is shown in the case of the discoveries above described, from profiting by them in peace. Hence they ought not to claim any rights if they themselves make no contributions, and their reasons for doing so are weak and foolish.

To prove more conclusively that they who maintain this position do so without any foundation, let us suppose that a Spaniard or other foreigner had discovered lands and wealth at the expense of the King of France. Could the Spaniards or other foreigners claim these discoveries and this wealth on the ground that the discoverer was a Spaniard or foreigner? No! There would be no sense in doing so, and they would always belong to France. Hence the people of St. Malo cannot make these claims for the reason which they give, that Cartier was a citizen of their city; and they can only take cognizance of the fact that he was a citizen of theirs, and render him accordingly the praise which is his due.

Besides, Cartier in the voyage which he made never passed the great fall of St. Louis, and made no discoveries north or south of the river St. Lawrence. His narratives give no evidence of it, in which he speaks only of the river Saguenay, the Trois Rivières and St. Croix, where he spent the winter in a fort near our settlement. Had he done so, he would not have failed to mention it, any more than what he has mentioned, which shows that he left all the upper part of the St. Lawrence, from Tadoussac to the great fall, being a territory difficult to explore, and that he was unwilling to expose himself or let his barques engage in the venture. So that what he did has borne no fruit until four years ago, when we made our settlement at Quebec, after which I ventured to pass the fall to help the savages in their wars, and fend among them men to make the acquaintance of the people, to learn their mode of living, and the character and extent of their territory. After devoting ourselves to labors which have been so successful, is it not just that we should enjoy their fruits, His Majesty not having contributed anything to aid those who have assumed the responsibilities of these undertakings up to the present time. I hope that God will at some time incline him to do so much for His service, his own glory and the welfare of his subjects, as to bring many new peoples to the knowledge of our faith, that they may at last enjoy the heavenly kingdom.

NOTE.

Champlain here introduces an explanation of his two geographical maps of New France, and likewise his method of determining a meridian line. For convenience of use the maps are placed at the end of this work, and for the same reason these explanations are carried forward to p. 219, in immediate proximity to the maps which they explain.—EDITOR.

ENDNOTES:

23. De Monts was governor of Pons, a town situated about ten miles south of Saintes, in the present department of Lower Charente.

24. *Ochateguins. Vide* Vol III. Quebec ed. p 169. They were Hurons, and
Ochateguin is supposed to have been one of their chiefs. *Vide* Vol II. note 321.

FOURTH VOYAGE OF SIEUR DE CHAMPLAIN,

CAPTAIN IN ORDINARY TO THE KING IN THE MARINE, AND LIEUTENANT OF MONSEIGNEUR LE PRINCE DE CONDÉ IN NEW FRANCE,

MADE IN THE YEAR 1613.

To the very high, powerful, and excellent Henri de Bourbon, Prince de
Condé, First Prince of the Blood, First Peer of France, Governor and Lieutenant of His Majesty in Guienne.

_Monseigneur,

The Honor that I have received from your Highness in being intrusted with the discovery of New France has inspired in me the desire to pursue with still greater pains and zeal than ever the search for the North Sea. With this object in view I have made a voyage during the past year, 1613, relying on a man whom I had sent there and who assured me he had seen it, as you will perceive in this brief narrative, which I venture to present to your Excellence, and in which are particularly described all the toils and sufferings I have had in the undertaking. But although I regret having lost this year so far as the main object is concerned, yet my expectation, as in the first voyage, of obtaining more definite information respecting the subject from the savages, has been fulfilled. They have told me about various lakes and rivers in the north, in view of which, aside from their assurance that they know of this sea, it seems to me easy to conclude from the maps that it cannot be far from the farthest discoveries I have hitherto made. Awaiting a favorable time and opportunity to prosecute my plans, and praying God to preserve you, most happy Prince, in all prosperity, wherein consists my highest wish for your greatness, I remain in the quality of

Your most humble and devoted servant,

SAMUEL DE CHAMPLAIN_.

FOURTH VOYAGE OF SIEUR DE CHAMPLAIN,

CAPTAIN IN ORDINARY TO THE KING IN THE MARINE, AND LIEUTENANT OF MONSEIGNEUR LE PRINCE DE CONDÉ IN NEW FRANCE,

MADE IN THE YEAR 1613.

CHAPTER I.

WHAT LED ME TO SEEK FOR TERMS OF REGULATION. – A COMMISSION OBTAINED – OPPOSITIONS TO THE SAME. – PUBLICATION AT LAST IN ALL THE PORTS OF FRANCE.

The desire which I have always had of making new discoveries in New France, for the good, profit, and glory of the French name, and at the same time to lead the poor natives to the knowledge of God, has led me to seek more and more for the greater facility of this undertaking, which can only be secured by means of good regulations. For, since individuals desire to gather the fruits of my labor without contributing to the expenses and great outlays requisite for the support of the settlements necessary to a successful result, this branch of trade is ruined by the greediness of gain, which is so great that it causes merchants to set out prematurely in order to arrive first in this country. By this means they not only become involved in the ice, but also in their own ruin, for, from trading with the savages in a secret manner and offering through rivalry with each other more merchandise than is necessary, they get the worst of the bargain. Thus, while purposing to deceive their associates, they generally deceive themselves.

For this reason, when I returned to France on the 10th of September, 1611, I spoke to Sieur de Monts about the matter, who approved of my suggestions; but his engagements not allowing him to prosecute the matter at court, he left to me its whole management.

I then drew up a statement, which I presented to President Jeannin, who, being a man desirous of seeing good undertakings prosper, commended my project, and encouraged me in its prosecution.

But feeling assured that those who love to fish in troubled waters would be vexed at such regulations and seek means to thwart them, it seemed advisable to throw myself into the hands of some power whose authority would prevail over their jealousy.

Now, knowing Monseigneur le Comte de Soissons[25] to be a prince devout and well disposed to all holy undertakings, I addressed myself to him through Sieur de Beaulieu, councillor, and almoner in ordinary to the King, and urged upon him the importance of the matter, setting forth the means of regulating it, the harm which disorder had heretofore produced, and the total ruin with which it was threatened, to the great dishonor of the French name, unless God should raise up some one who would reanimate it and give promise of securing for it some day the success which had hitherto been little anticipated. After he had been informed in regard to all the details of the scheme and seen the map of the country which I had made, he promised me, under the sanction of the King, to undertake the protectorate of the enterprise.

I immediately after presented to His Majesty, and to the gentlemen of his Council, a petition accompanied by articles, to the end that it might please him to issue regulations for the undertaking, without which, as I have said, it would fail. Accordingly his Majesty gave the direction and control to the before-mentioned Count, who then honored me with the lieutenancy.

Now as I was preparing to publish the commission [26] of the King in all the ports and harbors of France, there occurred the sickness and greatly lamented death of the Count, which postponed somewhat the undertaking. But his Majesty at once committed the direction to Monseigneur le Prince,[27] who proceeded in the execution of its duties, and, having in like manner honored me with the lieutenancy, [28] directed me to go on with the publication of the commission. But as soon as this was done, some marplots, who had no interest in the matter, importuned him to annul it, representing to him as they claimed the interests of all the merchants of France, who had no cause for complaint, since all were received into the association and could not therefore justly be aggrieved. Accordingly, their evil intention being recognized, they were dismissed, with permission only to enter into the association.

During these altercations, it was impossible for me, as the time of my departure was very near at hand, to do anything for the habitation at Quebec, for repairing and enlarging which I desired to take out some workmen. It was accordingly necessary to go out this year without any farther organization. The passports of Monseigneur le Prince were made out for four vessels, which were already in readiness for the voyage, viz. three from Rouen and one from La Rochelle, on condition that each should furnish four men for my assistance, not only in my discoveries but in war, as I desired to keep the promise which I had made to the Ochataiguins [29] in the year 1611, to assist them in their wars at the time of my next voyage.

As I was preparing to set out, I was informed that the Parliamentary Court of Rouen would not permit the publication of the commission of the King, because his Majesty had reserved to himself and his Council the sole cognizance of the differences which might arise in this matter; added to which was the fact that the merchants of St. Malo were also opposed to it. This greatly embarrassed me, and obliged me to make three journeys to Rouen, with orders of his Majesty, in consideration of which the Court desisted from their inhibition, and the assumptions of the opponents were overruled. The commission was then published in all the ports of Normandy.

ENDNOTES:

25. For a brief notice of the Count de Soissons, *vide* Vol. I. note 74; also note by Laverdière, Quebec ed., p. 433.

26. This Commission, dated October 15, 1612, will be found in Champlain's
issue of 1632. *Vide* Quebec ed., p 887.

27. Henry de Bourbon. *Vide* Vol. I. p 113, note 75.

28. Champlain was appointed lieutenant of the Prince de Condé on the 22d day of November, 1612. *Vide* issue of 1632, Quebec ed., p. 1072.

29. Ochateguins, or Hurons.

CHAPTER II.

DEPARTURE FROM FRANCE.—WHAT TOOK PLACE UP TO OUR ARRIVAL AT THE FALLS.

I set out from Rouen on the 5th of March for Honfleur, accompanied by Sieur L'Ange, to assist me in my explorations, and in war if occasion should require.

On the next day, the 6th of the month, we embarked in the vessel of Sieur de Pont Gravé, immediately setting sail, with a favorable wind.

On the 10th of April we sighted the Grand Bank, where we several times tried for fish, but without success.

On the 15th we had a violent gale, accompanied by rain and hail, which was followed by another, lasting forty-eight hours, and so violent as to cause the loss of several vessels on the island of Cape Breton.

On the 21st we sighted the island and Cap de Raye. [30] On the 29th the Montagnais savages, perceiving us from All Devils' Point, [31] threw themselves into their canoes and came to meet us, being so thin and hideous-looking that I did not recognize them. At once they began crying for bread, saying that they were dying of hunger. This led us to conclude that the winter had not been severe, and consequently the hunting poor, which matter we have alluded to in previous voyages.

Having arrived on board of our vessel they examined the faces of all, and as I was not to be seen anywhere they asked where Monsieur de Champlain was, and were answered that I had remained in France. But this they would not think of believing, and an old man among them came to me in a corner where I was walking, not desiring to be recognized as yet, and taking me by the ear, for he suspected who it was, saw the scar of the arrow wound, which I received at the defeat of the Iroquois. At this he cried out, and all the others after him, with great demonstrations of joy, saying, Your people are awaiting you at the harbor of Tadoussac.

The same day we arrived at Tadoussac, and although we had set out last, nevertheless arrived first, Sieur Boyer of Rouen arriving with the same tide. From this it is evident that to set out before the season is simply rushing into the ice. When we had anchored, our friends came out to us, and, after informing us how everything was at the habitation, began to dress three *outardes* [32] and two hares, which they had brought, throwing the entrails overboard, after which the poor savages rushed, and, like famished beasts, devoured them without drawing. They also scraped off with their nails the fat with which our vessel had been coated, eating it gluttonously as if they had found some great delicacy.

The next day two vessels arrived from St. Malo, which had set out before the oppositions had been settled and the commission been published in Normandy. I proceeded on board, accompanied by L'Ange. The Sieurs de la Moinerie and la Tremblaye were in command, to whom I read the commission of the King, and the prohibition against violating it on penalties attached to the same. They replied that they were subjects and faithful servants of His Majesty, and that they would obey his commands; and I then had attached to a post in the port the arms and commission of His Majesty, that no ground for ignorance might be claimed.

On the 2d of May, seeing two shallops equipped to go to the Falls, I embarked with the before-mentioned L'Ange in one of them. We had very bad weather, so that the masts of our shallop were broken, and had it not been for the preserving hand of God we should have been lost, as was before our eyes a shallop from St Malo, which was going to the Isle d'Orleans, those on board of which however being saved.

On the 7th we arrived at Quebec, where we found in good condition those who had wintered there, they not having been sick; they told us that the winter had not been severe, and that the river had not frozen. The trees also were beginning to put forth leaves and the fields to be decked with flowers.

On the 13th we set out from Quebec for the Falls of St. Louis, where we arrived on the 21st, finding there one of, our barques which had set out after us from Tadoussac, and which had traded some with a small troop of Algonquins, who came from the war with the Iroquois, and had with them two prisoners. Those in the barque gave them to understand that I had come with a number of men to assist them in their wars, according to the promise I had made them in previous years; also that I desired to go to their country and enter into an alliance with all their friends, at which they were greatly pleased. And, inasmuch as they were desirous of returning to their country to assure their friends of their victory, see their wives, and put to death their prisoners in a festive *tabagie*, they left us pledges of their return, which they promised should be before the middle of the first moon, according to their reckoning, their shields made of wood and elk leather, and a part of their bows and arrows. I regretted very much that I was not prepared to go with them to their country.

Three days after, three canoes arrived with Algonquins, who had come from the interior, with some articles of merchandise which they bartered. They told me that the bad treatment which the savages had received the year before had discouraged them from coming any more, and that they did not believe that I would ever return to their country on account of the wrong impressions which those jealous of me had given them respecting me; wherefore twelve hundred men had gone to the war, having no more hope from the French, who, they did not believe, would return again to their country.

This intelligence greatly disheartened the merchants, as they had made a great purchase of merchandise, with the expectation that the savages would come, as they had been accustomed to. This led me to resolve, as I engaged in my explorations, to pass through their country, in order to encourage those who had stayed back, with an assurance of the good treatment they would receive, and of the large amount of good merchandise at the Fall, and also of the desire I had to assist them in their war. For carrying out this purpose I requested three canoes and three savages to guide us, but after much difficulty obtained only two and one savage, and this by means of some presents made them.

ENDNOTES:

30. The *island* refers to New Foundland. Cap de Raye, still known as Cape

Ray, was on the southwestern angle of New Foundland.

31. Now called Point aux Vaches. It was sometimes called All-Devils'

Point. *Vide* note 136, Vol. I. p. 235.

32. *Outardes*. Sometimes written *houtardes,* and *Oltardes*. The name outarde or bustard, the *otis* of ornithologists, a land bird of Europe, was applied to a species of goose in Canada at a very early period.

> The outarde is mentioned by Cartier in 1535, and the name may have been originally applied by the fishermen and fur-traders at a much earlier period, doubtless on account of some fancied resemblance which they saw to the lesser bustard or outarde, which was about the size of the English pheasant. *Vide Pennant's British Zoölogy,* Vol. I. p. 379. Cartier, Champlain, Lescarbot, Baron La Hontan, Potherie, and Charlvoix mention the outarde in catalogues of water-fowl in which *oye,* the goose, is likewise mentioned. They very clearly distinguish it from the class which they commonly considered *oyes,* or geese. Cartier, for instance, says, Il y a aussi grand nombre d'oyseaulx, scauoir grues, signes, *oltardes, oyes sauuages, blanches, & grises*. Others speak of *outardes et oyes*. They do not generally describe it with particularity. Champlain, however, in describing the turkey, *cocq d'Inde,* on the coast of New England, says, *aussi gros qu'vne outarde, qui est une espece d'oye*. Father Pierre Biard writes, *et au mesme temps les outardes arriuent du midy, qui sont grosses cannes au double des nostres*. From these statements it is obvious that the outarde was a species of goose, but was so small that it could well be described as a large duck. In New France there were at least four species of the goose,

which might have come under the observation of the early navigators and explorers. We give them in the order of their size, as described in Coues' Key to North American Birds.

1. Canada Goose, *Branta Canadensis*, SCOPOLI, 36 inches.
2. Snow Goose, *Anser hyperboreus*, LINNÆUS, 30 inches.
3. Am. White-fronted Goose, *Anser albifrons*, LINNÆUS, 27 inches.
4. Brant Goose, *Branta bernicla*, SCOPOLI, 24 inches.

Recurring to the statement of Cartier above cited, it will be observed that he mentions, besides the outarde, wild geese white and gray. The first and largest of the four species above mentioned, the Canada goose, *Branta Canadensis*, is gray, and the two next, the Snow goose and White-fronted, would be classified as white. This disposes of three of the four mentioned. The outarde of Cartier would therefore be the fourth species in the list, viz. the Brant goose. *Branta bernicla*. This is the smallest species found on our northern coast, and might naturally be described, as stated by Father Biard, as a large duck. It is obvious that the good Father could not have described the Canada goose, the largest of the four species, as a large duck, and the white geese have never been supposed to be referred to under the name of outarde. The Brant goose, to which all the evidence which we have been able to find in the Canadian authorities seems to point as the outarde of early times, is common in our markets in its season, but our marketmen, unaccustomed to make scientific distinctions, are puzzled to decide whether it should be classed as a goose or a duck. It is not improbable that the early voyagers to our northern latitudes, unable to decide to which of these classes this water-fowl properly belonged, and seeing in it a fancied resemblance to the lesser outarde, with which they were familiar, gave it for sake of the distinction, but nevertheless inappropriately, the name of outarde. The reader is referred to the following authorities.

Vide Brief Récit par Jacques Cartier, 1545. D'Avezac ed., p. 33; *Champlain*, Quebec ed., p. 220; *Jésuite Relations*, 1616, p. 10; *Le Grand Voyage du Pays des Hurons*, par Sagard, Paris, 1632, p. 301; *Dictionaire de la Langue Hurone*, par Sagard, Paris, 1632, *oyseaux; Letters to the Dutchess of Lesdiguieres*, By Fr. Xa. de Charlevoix, London. 1763, p. 88; *Le Jeune, Relations des Jésuites*, 1633, P. 4, 1636, p. 47; *Histoire de l'Amérique Septentrionale*, par de la Potherie, Paris, 1722, Vol. I. pp. 20, 172, 212, 308; *Lescarbot, Histoire de la Nouvelle France*, pp. 369, 582, 611.

CHAPTER III.

DEPARTURE TO DISCOVER THE NORTH SEA, ON THE GROUND OF THE REPORT MADE ME IN REGARD TO IT. DESCRIPTION OF SEVERAL RIVERS, LAKES AND ISLANDS, THE FALLS OF THE CHAUDIÈRE AND OTHER FALLS.

Now, as I had only two canoes, I could take with me but four men, among whom was one named Nicholas de Vignau, the most impudent liar that has been seen for a long time, as the sequel of this narrative will show. He had formerly spent the winter with the savages, and I had sent him on explorations the preceding years. He reported to me, on his return to Paris in 1612, that he had seen the North Sea; that the river of the Algonquins came from a lake which emptied into it; and that in seventeen days one could go from the Falls of St. Louis to this sea and back again; that he had seen the wreck and *débris* of an English ship that had been wrecked, on board of which were eighty men, who had escaped to the shore, and whom the savages killed because the English endeavored to take from them by force their Indian corn and other necessaries of life; and that he had seen the scalps which these savages had flayed off, according to their custom, which they would show me, and that they would likewise give me a young English boy whom they had kept for me. This intelligence had greatly pleased me, for I thought that I had almost found that for which I had for a long time been searching. Accordingly I enjoined upon him to tell me the truth, in order that I might inform the King, and warned him that if he gave utterance to a lie he was putting the rope about his neck, assuring him on the other hand that, if his narrative were true, he could be certain of being well rewarded. He again assured me, with stronger oaths than ever; and in order to play his *rôle* better he gave me a description of the country, which he said he had made as well as he was able. Accordingly the confidence which I saw in him, his entire frankness as it seemed, the description which he had prepared, the wreck and *debris* of the ship, and the things above mentioned, had an appearance of probability, in connection with the voyage of the English to Labrador in 1612, where they found a strait, in which they sailed as far as the 63d degree of latitude and the 290th of longitude, wintering at the 53d degree and losing some vessels, as their report proves.[33] These circumstances inducing me to believe that what he said was true, I made a report of the same to the Chancellor, [34] which I showed to Marshal de Brissac,[35] President Jeannin, [36] and other Seigneurs of the Court, who told me that I ought to visit the place in person. For this reason I requested Sieur Georges, a merchant of La Rochelle, to give him a passage in his ship, which he willingly did, and during the voyage he questioned him as to his object in making it; and, since it was not of any profit to him, he asked if he expected any pay, to which the young man answered that he did not, that he did not expect anything, from any one but the King, and that he undertook the voyage only to show me the North Sea, which he had seen. He made an affidavit of this at La Rochelle before two notaries.

Now as I took leave on Whitsuntide, [37] of all the principal men to whose prayers I commended myself, and also to those of all others, I said to him in their presence that if what he had previously said was not true he must not give me the trouble to undertake the journey, which involved many dangers. Again he affirmed all that he had said, on peril of his life.

Accordingly, our canoes being laden with some provisions, our arms, and a few articles of merchandise for making presents to the savages, I set out on Monday the 27th of May from Isle St. Hélène with four Frenchmen and one savage, a parting salute being given me with some rounds from small pieces. This day we went only to the Falls of St. Louis, a league up the river, the bad weather not allowing us to go any farther.

On the 29th we passed the Falls, [38] partly by land, partly by water, it being necessary for us to carry our canoes, clothes, victuals, and arms on our shoulders, no small matter for persons not accustomed to it. After going two leagues beyond the Falls, we entered a lake, [39] about twelve leagues in circuit, into which three rivers empty; one coming from the west, from the direction of the Ochateguins, distant from one hundred and fifty to two hundred leagues from the great Falls; [40] another from the south and the country of the Iroquois, a like distance off; [41] and the other from the north and the country of the Algonquins and Nebicerini, also about the same distance. [42] This river on the north, according to the report of the savages, comes from a source more remote, and passes by tribes unknown to them and about three hundred leagues distant.

This lake is filled with fine large islands, containing only pasturage land, where there is fine hunting, deer and fowl being plenty. Fish are abundant. The country bordering the lake is covered with extensive forests. We proceeded to pass the night at the entrance to this lake, making barricades against the Iroquois, who roam in these regions in order to surprise their enemies; and I am sure that if they were to find us they would give us as good a welcome as them, for which reason we kept a good watch all night. On the next day I took the altitude of the place, and found it in latitude 45° 18'. About three o'clock in the afternoon we entered the river which comes from the north, and, passing a small fall [43] by land so as to favor our canoes, we proceeded to a little island, where we spent the remainder of the night.

On the last day of May we passed another lake, [44] seven or eight leagues long and three broad, containing several islands. The neighboring country is very level, except in some places, where there are pine-covered hills. We passed a fall called by the inhabitants of the country Quenechouan,[45] which is filled with stones and rocks, and where the water runs with great velocity. We had to get into the water and drag our canoes along the shore with a rope. Half a league from there we passed another little fall by rowing, which makes one sweat. Great skill is required in passing these falls, in order to avoid the eddies and surf, in which they abound; but the savages do this with the greatest possible dexterity, winding about and going by the easiest places, which they recognize at a glance.

On Saturday, the 1st of June, we passed two other falls; the first half a league long, the second a league, in which we had much difficulty; for the rapidity of the current is so great that it makes a frightful noise, and produces, as it descends from stage to stage, so white a foam everywhere that the water cannot be seen at all. This fall is strewn with rocks, and contains some islands here and there covered with pines and white cedars. This was the place where we had a hard time; for, not being able to carry our canoes by land on account of the density of the wood, we had to drag them in the water with ropes, and in drawing mine I came near losing my life, as it crossed into one of the eddies, and if I had not had the good fortune to fall between two rocks the canoe would have dragged me in, inasmuch as I was unable to undo quickly enough the rope which was wound around my hand, and which hurt me severely and came near cutting it off. In this danger I cried to God and began to pull my canoe, which was returned to me by the refluent water, such as occurs in these falls. Having thus escaped I thanked God, begging Him to preserve us. Later our savage came to help me, but I was out of danger. It is not strange that I was desirous of preserving my canoe, for if it had been lost it would have been necessary to remain, or wait until some savages came that way, a poor hope for those who have nothing to dine on, and who are not accustomed to such hardship. As for our Frenchmen, they did not have any better luck, and several times came near losing their lives; but the Divine Goodness preserved us all. During the remainder of the day we rested, having done enough.

The next day we fell in with fifteen canoes of savages called *Quenongebin,* [46] in a river, after we had passed a small lake, four leagues long and two broad. They had been informed of my coming by those who had passed the Falls of St. Louis, on their way from the war with the Iroquois. I was very glad to meet them, as were they also to meet me, but they were astonished to see me in this country with so few companions, and with only one savage. Accordingly, after saluting each other after the manner of the country, I desired them not to go any farther until I had informed them of my plan. To this they assented, and we encamped on an island.

The next day I explained to them that I was on my way to their country to visit them, and fulfil the promise I had previously made them, and that if they had determined to go to the war it would be very agreeable to me, inasmuch as I had brought some companions with this view, at which they were greatly pleased; and having told them that I wished to go farther in order to notify the other tribes, they wanted to deter me, saying that the way was bad, and that we had seen nothing up to this point. Wherefore I asked them to give me one of their number to take charge of our second canoe, and also to serve us as guide, since our conductors were not acquainted any farther. This they did willingly, and in return I made them a present and gave them one of our Frenchmen, the least indispensable, whom I sent back to the Falls with a leaf of my note-book, on which for want of paper I made a report of myself.

Thus we parted, and continuing our course up the river we found another one, very fair and broad, which comes from a nation called *Ouescharini,* [47] who live north of it, a distance of four days' journey from the mouth. This river is very pleasant in consequence of the fine islands it contains, and the fair and open woods with which its shores are bordered. The land is very good for tillage.

On the fourth day we passed near another river coming from the north, where tribes called *Algonquins* live. This river falls into the great river St. Lawrence, three leagues below the Falls of St. Louis, forming a large island of nearly forty leagues. [48] This river is not broad, but filled with a countless number of falls, very hard to pass. Sometimes these tribes go by way of this river in order to avoid encounters with their enemies, knowing that they will not try to find them in places so difficult of access.

Where this river has its debouchure is another coming from the south, [49] at the mouth of which is a marvellous fall. For it descends a height of twenty or twenty-five fathoms [50] with such impetuosity that it makes an arch nearly four hundred paces broad. The savages take pleasure in passing under it, not wetting themselves, except from the spray that is thrown off. There is an island in the middle of the river which, like all the country round about, is covered with pines and white cedars. When the savages desire to enter the river they ascend the mountain, carrying their canoes, and go half a league by land. The neighboring country is filled with all sorts of game, so that the savages often make a stop here. The Iroquois also go there sometimes and surprise them while making the passage.

We passed a fall [51] a league from there, which is half a league broad, and has a descent of six or seven fathoms. There are many little islands, which are, however, nothing more than rough and dangerous rocks covered with a poor sort of brushwood. The water falls in one place with such force upon a rock that it has hollowed out in course of time a large and deep basin, in which the water has a circular motion and forms large eddies in the middle, so that the savages call it *Asticou*, which signifies boiler. This cataract produces such a noise in this basin that it is heard for more than two leagues. The savages when passing here observe a ceremony which we shall speak of in its place. We had much trouble in ascending by rowing against a strong current, in order to reach the foot of the fall. Here the savages took their canoes, my Frenchmen and myself, our arms, provisions, and other necessaries, and we passed over the rough rocks for the distance of about a quarter of a league, the extent of the fall. Then we embarked, being obliged afterwards to land a second time and go about three hundred paces through copse-wood, after which we got into the water in order to get our canoes over the sharp rocks, the trouble attending which may be imagined. I took the altitude of this place, which I found to be in latitude 45° 38'. [52]

In the afternoon we entered a lake, [53] five leagues long and two wide, in which there are very fine islands covered with vines, nut-trees, and other excellent kinds of trees. Ten or twelve leagues above we passed some islands covered with pines. The land is sandy, and there is found here a root which dyes a crimson color, with which the savages paint their faces, as also little gewgaws after their manner. There is also a mountain range along this river, and the surrounding country seems to be very unpromising. The rest of the day we passed on a very pleasant island.

The next day we proceeded on our course to a great fall, nearly three leagues broad, in which the water falls a height of ten or twelve fathoms in a slope, making a marvellous noise. [54] It is filled with a vast number of islands, covered with pines and cedars. In order to pass it we were obliged to give up our maize or Indian corn, and some few other provisions we had, together with our least necessary clothes, retaining only our arms and lines, to afford us means of support from hunting and fishing as place and luck might permit. Thus lightened we passed, sometimes rowing, sometimes carrying our canoes and arms by land, the fall, which is a league and a half long, [55] and in which our savages, who are indefatigable in this work and accustomed to endure such hardships, aided us greatly.

Continuing our course, we passed two other falls, one by land, the other with oar and poles standing up. Then we entered a lake, [56] six or seven leagues long, into which flows a river coming from the south, [57] on which at a distance of five days' journey from the other river [58] live a people called *Matou-oüescarini* [59] The lands about the before-mentioned lake are sandy and covered with pines, which have been almost entirely burned down by the savages. There are some islands, in one of which we rested ourselves. Here we saw a number of fine red cypresses,[60] the first I had seen in this country, out of which I made a cross, which I planted at one end of the island, on an elevated and conspicuous spot, with the arms of France, as I had done in other places where we had stopped. I called this island *Sainte Croix*.

On the 6th we set out from this island of St. Croix, where the river is a league and a half broad, and having made eight or ten leagues we passed a small fall by oar, and a number of islands of various sizes. Here our savages left the sacks containing their provisions and their less necessary articles, in order to be lighter for going overland and avoiding several falls which it was necessary to pass. There was a great dispute between our savages and our impostor, who affirmed that there was no danger by way of the falls, and that we ought to go that way. Our savages said to him, You are tired of living, and to me, that I ought not to believe him, and that he did not tell the truth. Accordingly, having several times observed that he had no knowledge of the places, I followed the advice of the savages, which was fortunate for me, for he fought for dangers in order to ruin me or to disgust me with the undertaking, as he has since confessed, a statement of which will be given hereafter. We crossed accordingly towards the west the river, which extended northward. I took the altitude of this place and found it in latitude 46° 40'.[61] We had much difficulty in going this distance overland. I, for my part, was loaded only with three arquebuses, as many oars, my cloak, and some small articles. I cheered on our men, who were somewhat more heavily loaded, but more troubled by the mosquitoes than by their loads. Thus after passing four small ponds and having gone a distance of two and a half leagues, we were so wearied that it was impossible to go farther, not having eaten for twenty-four hours anything but a little broiled fish without seasoning, for we had left our provisions behind, as I mentioned before. Accordingly we rested on the border of a pond, which was very pleasant, and made a fire to drive away the mosquitoes, which annoyed us greatly, whose persistency is so marvellous that one cannot describe it. Here we cast our lines to catch some fish.

The next day we passed this pond, which was perhaps a league long. Then we went by land three leagues through a country worse than we had yet seen, since the winds had blown down the pines on top of each other. This was no slight inconvenience, as it was necessary to go now over, now under, these trees. In this way we reached a lake, six leagues long and two wide, [62] very abundant in fish, the neighboring people doing their fishing there. Near this lake is a settlement of savages, who till the soil and gather harvests of maize. Their chief is named *Nibachis*, who came to visit us with his followers, astonished that we could have passed the falls and bad roads in order to reach them. After offering us tobacco, according to their custom, he began to address his companions, saying, that we must have fallen from the clouds, for he knew not how we could have made the journey, and that they who lived in the country had much trouble in traversing these bad ways: and he gave them to understand that I accomplished all that I set my mind upon; in short, that he believed respecting me all that the other savages had told him.

Aware that we were hungry, he gave us some fish, which we ate, and after our meal I explained to him, through Thomas, our interpreter, the pleasure I had in meeting them, that I had come to this country to assist them in their wars, and that I desired to go still farther to see some other chiefs for the same object, at which they were glad and promised me assistance. They showed me their gardens and the fields, where they had maize. Their soil is sandy, for which reason they devote themselves more to hunting than to tillage, unlike the Ochateguins. [63] When they wish to make a piece of land arable, they burn down the trees, which is very easily done, as they are all pines, and filled with rosin. The trees having been burned, they dig up the ground a little, and plant their maize kernel by kernel, [64] like those in Florida. At the time I was there it was only four fingers high.

ENDNOTES:

33. *Vide* Vol. II. p. 171, note 297, for an account of Henry Hudson, to whom this statement refers. De Vignau had undoubtedly heard rumors concerning Hudson's expedition to the bay that bears his name in the years 1610-11, out of which he fabricated the fine story of his pretended discovery. Longitude at that time was reckoned from the island of Ferro, one of the Canaries. Proceeding from west to east, the 290° would pass through Hudson's Bay, as may be seen by consulting any early French map. *Vide* Bellin's *Carte du Globe Terrestre*, 1764.

34. Nicholas Brulart de Sillery, who was born at Sillery, in France, in 1544, and died in the same place in 1624. He rendered signal service to Henry IV. Among other public acts he negotiated the peace of Vervins between France and Spain in 1598. He was appointed grand chancellor of France in 1607. Henry IV. said of him, Avec mon chanclier qui ne fait pas le latin et mon connetable (Henri de Montmorency), qui ne fait ni lire ni écrire, je puis venir à bout des affairs les plus difficiles.

35. For some account of Marshal de Brissac, *vide* Vol. I. p. 17, note 16.

36. *Vide* Vol. I. p. 112, note 73. President Jeannin was a most suitable person to consult on this subject, as he was deeply interested in

the discovery of a northwest passage to India. When minister at the Hague he addressed a letter bearing date January 21st, 1609, to Henry IV. of France, containing an account of his indirect negotiations with Henry Hudson, for a voyage to discover a shorter passage to India. A copy of this interesting letter, both in French and English, may be found in *Henry Hudson the Navigator*, by G. M. Asher, LL.D., Hakluyt Society, London, 1860, p. 244.

37. The festival of Whitsunday occurred on the 26th May. *Laverdière in loco.*

38. The Falls of St Louis.

39. Lake St. Louis.

40. Champlain is here speaking of the river St. Lawrence, which flows into Lake St. Louis slightly south of west.

41. Rivière de Loup, now known as the Chateauguay.

42. The River Ottawa or a branch of it flows into Lake St. Louis from the north, although its course is rather from the west. It was often called the River of the Algonquins. It approaches comparatively near to Lake Nipissing, the home of the Nipissirini. The sources of the Ottawa are northeast of Lake Nipissing, a distance of from one to three hundred miles. The distances here given by Champlain are only general estimates gathered from the Indians, and are necessarily inaccurate.

43. Rapide de Brussi, by which the river flows from the Lake of Two Mountains into Lake St Louis.

44. *Lac de Soissons*, now called Lake of Two Mountains *Vide* Vol. I. p. 294.

45. This is the first of a series of falls now known as the Long Fall.

46. *Quenongebin*. Laverdière makes, this the same as the Kinounchepiríni of Vimont. It was an Algonquin nation situated south of Allumette Island. *Vide Jesuite Relations*, Quebec ed, 1640, p. 34.

47. *Ouescharini*. These people, called Ouaouechkairini by Vimont, appear to have dwelt on the stream now known as the *Rivière de*

Petite Nation, rising in a system of lakes, among which are Lake Simon, Whitefish Lake, Long Lake, and Lake Des Isles. *Vide Jesuite Relations,* 1640, p. 34. The tribe here mentioned was subsequently called the Little Nation of the Algonquins hence the name of the river. *Laverdière.*

48. This passage is exceedingly obscure. Laverdière supposes that part of a sentence was left out by the printer. If so it is remarkable that Champlain did not correct it in his edition of 1632. Laverdière thinks the river here spoken of is the Gatineau, and that the savages following up this stream went by a portage to the St. Maurice, and passing down reached the St. Lawrence *thirty* leagues, and not *three,* below the Falls of Saint Louis. The three rivers thus named inclose or form an island of about the extent described in the text. This explanation is plausible. The passage amended would read, "This river *extends near another which* falls into the great river St. Lawrence thirty leagues below the falls of St. Louis." We know of no other way in which the passage can be rationally explained.

49. Rideau, at the mouth of which is Green Island, referred to in the text below.

50. The fall in the Rideau is thirty-four feet, according to the Edinburgh Gazetteer of the World. The estimate of Champlain is so far out of the way that it seems not unlikely that feet were intended instead of fathoms. *Vide* Vol. I. pp. 301, 302.

51. The Chaudière Falls, just above the present city of Ottawa, the greatest height of which is about forty feet "Arrayed in every imaginable variety of form, in vast dark masses, in graceful cascades, or in tumbling spray, they have been well described as a hundred rivers struggling for a passage. Not the least interesting feature they present is the Lost Chaudière, where a large body of water is quietly sucked down, and disappears underground" *Vide Canada* by W. H Smith. Vol. I. p. 120. Also Vol I. p, 120 of this work.

52. The latitude of the Chaudière Falls is about 45° 27'.

53. Chaudière Lake, which was only an expansion of the River Ottawa.

54. Rapide des Chats.

55. This probably refers to that part of the fall which was more difficult to pass.

56. Lake des Chats. The name *des chats* appears to have been given to this Lake, the Rapids, and the *Nation des chats*, on account of the great number of the *loup cervier*, or wild cats, *chats sauvages*, found in this region. Cf. *Le Grande Voyage du Pays des Hurons*, par Sagard, Paris, 1632, p. 307.

57. Madawaskca River, an affluent of the Ottawa, uniting with it at Fitz Roy.

58. Probably an allusion to the River St. Lawrence.

59. This is the same tribe alluded to by Vimont under the name *Mataouchkarmi*, as dwelling south of Allumette Island. *Vide Relations des Jésuites*, 1640, Quebec ed., p. 34.

60. Cyprés, Red Cedar or Savin, *Juniperus Virginiana*. *Vide* Vol. II. note 168.

61. They were now, perhaps, two miles below Portage du Fort, at the point on the Ottawa nearest to the system of lakes through which they were to pass, and where, as stated in the text, the Ottawa, making an angle, begins to flow directly from the north. The latitude, as here given, is even more than usually incorrect, being too high by more than a degree. The true latitude is about 43° 37'. *Vide Walker* and *Miles's Atlas of Dominion of Canada*. Note 62 will explain the cause of this inexactness.

62. Muskrat Lake. On Champlain's map of 1632 will be seen laid down a succession of lakes or ponds, together with the larger one, now known as Muskrat Lake, on the borders of which are figured the dwellings of the savages referred to in the text. The pond which they passed is the last in the series before reaching Muskrat Lake. On the direct route between this pond and the lake, known as the Muskrat Portage road, the course undoubtedly traversed by Champlain, there was found in 1867, in the, township of Ross, an astrolabe, an instrument used in taking latitudes, on which is the date, 1603. It is supposed to have been lost by Champlain on his present expedition. The reasons for this supposition have been stated in several brochures recently issued, one by Mr. O. H. Marshall of Buffalo, entitled *Discovery of an Astrolabe supposed to have been left by*

Champlain in 1613, New York, 1879; reprinted from the *Magazine of American History* for March of that year. Another, *Champlain's Astrolabe lost on the 7th of June, 1613, and found in August, 1867*, by A. J Russell of Ottawa, Montreal, 1879. And a third entitled *The Astrolabe of Samuel Champlain and Geoffrey Chaucer*, by Henry Scadding, D.D., of Toronto, 1880. All of these writers agree in the opinion that the instrument was probably lost by Champlain on his expedition up the Ottawa in 1613. For the argument *in extenso* the reader is referred to the brochures above cited.

[Illustration of an astrolabe.]

> Mr. Russell, who examined the astrolabe thus found with great care and had it photographed, describes it as a circular plate having a diameter of five inches and five eighths. "It is of place brass, very dark with age, one eighth of an inch thick above, increasing to six sixteenths of an inch below, to give it steadiness when suspended, which apparently was intended to be increased by hanging a weight on the little projecting ring at the bottom of it, in using it on shipboard. Its suspending ring is attached by a double hinge of the nature of a universal joint. Its circle is divided into single degrees, graduated from its perpendicular of suspension. The double-bladed index, the pivot of which passes through the centre of the astrolabe, has slits and eyelets in the projecting fights that are on it."
>
> We give on the preceding page an engraving of this astrolabe from a photograph, which presents a sufficiently accurate outline of the instrument. The plate was originally made to illustrate Mr. Marshall's article in the Magazine of American History, and we are indebted to the courtesy of the proprietors of the Magazine, Messrs. A. S. Barnes and Company of New York, for its use for our present purpose.
>
> The astrolabe, as an instrument for taking the altitude of the stars or the sun, had long been in use. Thomas Blundevile, who wrote in 1622, says he had

seen three kinds, and that the astrolabe of Stofflerus had then been in use a hundred years. It had been improved by Gemma Frisius. Mr. Blagrave had likewise improved upon the last-mentioned, and his instrument was at that time in general use in England. The astrolabe continued to be employed in Great Britain in taking altitudes for more than a century subsequent to this, certainly till Hadley's Quadrant was invented, which was first announced in 1731.

The astrolabes which had the broadest disks were more exact, as they were projected on a larger scale, but as they were easily jostled by the wind or the movement of the ship at sea, they could with difficulty be employed. But Mr. Blundevile informs us that "the Spaniards doe commonly make their astrolabes narrow and weighty, which for the most part are not much above five inches broad, and yet doe weigh at the least foure pound, & to that end the lower part is made a great deale thicker than the upper part towards the ring or handle." *Vide M. Blendeale his Exercises*, London, 1622, pp. 595, 597. This Spanish instrument, it will be observed, is very similar to that found on the Old Portage road, and the latter may have been of Spanish make.

In order to take the latitude in Champlain's day, at least three distinct steps or processes were necessary, and the following directions might have been given.

I. Let the astrolabe be suspended so that it shall hang plumb. Direct the index or diopter to the sun at noon, so that the same ray of light may shine through both holes in the two tablets or pinules on the diopter, and the diopter will point to the degree of the sun's meridian altitude indicated on the outer rim of the astrolabe.

II. Ascertain the exact degree of the sun's declination for that day, by a table calculated for that purpose, which accompanies the astrolabe.

III. Subtract the declination, so found, if it be northerly, from the meridian altitude; or if the declination be southerly, add the declination to the meridian altitude, and the result, subtracted from 90°, will give the latitude.

In these several processes of taking the latitude there are numerous possibilities of inexactness. It does not appear that any correction was made for refraction of light, or the precession of the equinoxes. But the most important source of inaccuracy was in the use of the astrolabe whose disk was so small that its divisions could not be carried beyond degrees, and consequently minutes were arrived at by sheer estimation, and usually when the work was completed, the error was not less than one fourth or one half of a degree, and it was often much more.

This accounts fully for the inaccuracies of Champlain's latitudes from first to last throughout his entire explorations, as tested by the very exact instruments and tables now in use. No better method of determining the latitude existed at that day, and consequently the historian is warned not to rely upon the latitude alone as given by the early navigators and explorers in identifying the exact localities which they visited.

63. Subsequently called Hurons.

64. *Vide* Vol. I. p. 49; Vol. II. note 219.

CHAPTER IV.

CONTINUATION.—ARRIVAL AT THE ABODE OF TESSOUAT, AND HIS FAVORABLE RECEPTION OF ME.—CHARACTER OF THEIR CEMETERIES—THE SAVAGES PROMISE ME FOUR CANOES FOR CONTINUING MY JOURNEY, WHICH THEY HOWEVER SHORTLY AFTER REFUSE.—

ADDRESS OF THE SAVAGES TO DISSUADE ME FROM MY UNDERTAKING, IN WHICH THEY REPRESENT ITS DIFFICULTIES – MY REPLY TO THESE OBJECTIONS. – TESSOUAT ACCUSES MY GUIDE OF LYING, AND OF NOT HAVING BEEN WHERE HE SAID HE HAD. – THE LATTER MAINTAINS HIS VERACITY – I URGE THEM TO GIVE ME CANOES. – SEVERAL REFUSALS. – MY GUIDE CONVICTED OF FALSEHOOD, AND HIS CONFESSION.

Nibachis had two canoes fitted out, to conduct me to another chief, named Tessoüat, [65] who lived eight leagues from him, on the border of a great lake, through which flows the river which we had left, and which extends northward. Accordingly we crossed the lake in a west-northwesterly direction, a distance of nearly seven leagues. Landing there, we went a league towards the northeast through a very fine country, where are small beaten paths, along which one can go easily. Thus we arrived on the shore of the lake, [66] where the dwelling of Tessoüat was. He was accompanied by a neighboring chieftain, and was greatly amazed to see me, saying that he thought I was a dream, and that he did not believe his eyes. Thence we crossed on to an island, [67] where their cabins are, which are poorly constructed out of the bark of trees. The island is covered with oaks, pines, and elms, and is not subject to inundations, like the other islands in the lake.

This island is strongly situated; for at its two ends, and where the river enters the lake, there are troublesome falls, the roughness of which makes the island difficult of access. They have accordingly taken up their abode here in order to avoid the pursuit of their enemies. It is in latitude 47°, [68] as also the lake, which is twenty leagues long, [69] and three or four wide. It abounds in fish; the hunting, however, is not especially good.

On visiting the island, I observed their cemeteries, and was struck with wonder as I saw sepulchres of a shape like shrines, made of pieces of wood fixed in the ground at a distance of about three feet from each other, and intersecting at the upper end. On the intersections above they place a large piece of wood, and in front another upright piece, on which is carved roughly, as would be expected, the figure of the male or female interred. If it is a man, they add a shield, a sword attached to a handle after their manner, a mace, and bow and arrows. If it is a chief, there is a plume on his head, and some other *matachia* or embellishment. If it is a child, they give it a bow and arrow; if a woman or girl, a boiler, an earthen vessel, a wooden spoon, and an oar. The entire sepulchre is six or seven feet long at most, and four wide; others are smaller. They are painted yellow and red, with various ornaments as neatly done as the carving. The deceased is buried with his dress of beaver or other skins which he wore when living, and they lay by his side all his possessions, as hatchets, knives, boilers, and awls, so that these things may serve him in the land whither he goes; for they believe in the immortality of the soul, as I have elsewhere observed. These carved sepulchres are only made for the warriors; for in respect to others they add no more than in the case of women, who are considered a useless class, accordingly but little is added in their case.

Observing the poor quality of the soil, I asked them what pleasure they took in cultivating land so unpromising, since there was some much better, which they left barren and waste, as at the Falls of St. Louis. They answered that they were forced to do so in order to dwell in security, and that the roughness of the locality served them as a defence against their enemies. But they said that if I would make a settlement of French at the Falls of St. Louis, as I had promised, they would leave their abode and go and live near us, confident that their enemies would do them no harm while we were with them. I told them that we would this year collect wood and stone in order the coming year to build a fort and cultivate the land; upon hearing which they raised a great cry of applause. This conference having been finished, I asked all the chiefs and prominent men among them to assemble the next day on the main land, at the cabin of Tessoüat, who purposed to celebrate a *tabagie* in my honor, adding that I would there tell them my plans. This they promised, and sent word to their neighbors to convene at the appointed place.

The next day all the guests came, each with his porringer and wooden spoon. They seated themselves without order or ceremony on the ground in the cabin of Tessoüat, who distributed to them a kind of broth made of maize crushed between two stones, together with meat and fish which was cut into little pieces, the whole being boiled together without salt. They also had meat roasted on coals, and fish boiled apart, which he also distributed. In respect to myself, as I did not wish any of their chowder, which they prepare in a very dirty manner, I asked them for some fish and meat, that I might prepare it in my own way, which they gave me. For drink, we had fine clear water. Tessoüat, who gave the *tabagie*, entertained us without eating himself, according to their custom.

The *tabagie* being over, the young men, who are not present at the harangues and councils, and who during the *tabagies* remain at the door of the cabins, withdrew, when all who remained began to fill their pipes, one and another offering me one. We then spent a full half-hour in this occupation, not a word being spoken, as is their custom.

After smoking amply during so long a period of silence, I explained to them, through my interpreter, that the object of my journey was none other than to assure them of my friendship, and of the desire I had to assist them in their wars, as I had before done; that I had been prevented from coming the preceding year, as I had promised them, because the king had employed me in other wars, but that now he had ordered me to visit them and to fulfil my promises, and that for this purpose I had a number of men at the Falls of St. Louis. I told them that I was making an excursion in their territory to observe the fertility of their soil, their lakes and rivers, and the sea which they had told me was in their country; and that I desired to see a tribe distant six days' journey from them, called the *Nebicerini*, in order to invite them also to the war, and accordingly I asked them to give me four canoes with eight savages to guide me to these lands. And since the Algonquins are not great friends of the *Nebicerini*, [70] they seemed to listen to me with greater attention.

After I had finished my discourse, they began again to smoke, and to confer among themselves in a very low voice respecting my propositions. Then Tessoüat in behalf of all the rest began and said, that they had always regarded me more friendly towards them than any Frenchman they had seen; that the proofs they had of this in the past made their confidence easier for the future: moreover, that I had shown myself in reality their friend, by encountering so many risks in coming to see them and invite them to the war, and that all these considerations obliged them to feel as kindly disposed towards me as towards their own children. But they said that I had the preceding year broken my promise, that two thousand savages had gone to the Falls with the expectation of finding me ready to go to the war, and making me presents, but that they had not found me and were greatly saddened, supposing that I was dead, as some persons had told them. He said also, that the French who were at the Falls did not want to help them in their wars, that they had been badly treated by certain ones, so that they had resolved among themselves not to go to the Falls again, and that this had caused them, as they did not expect to see me again, to go alone to the war, and that in fact twelve hundred of them had already gone. And since the greater part of their warriors were absent, they begged me to postpone the expedition to the following year, saying that they would communicate the matter to all the people of their country. In regard to the four canoes, which I asked for, they granted them to me, but with great reluctance, telling me that they were greatly displeased at the idea of such an undertaking, in view of the hardships which I would endure; that the people there were sorcerers, that they had caused the death of many of their own tribe by charms and poisoning, on which account they were not their friends: moreover they said that, as it regards war, I was not to think of them, as they were little-hearted. With these and many other considerations they endeavored to deter me from my purpose.

But my sole desire on the other hand was to see this people, and enter into friendship with them, so that I might visit the North Sea. Accordingly, with a view to lessening the force of their objections, I said to them, that it was not far to the country in question; that the bad roads could not be worse than those I had already passed; that their witchcraft would have no power to harm me, as my God would preserve me from them; that I was also acquainted with their herbs, and would therefore beware of eating them; that I desired to make the two tribes mutual friends, and that I would to this end make presents to the other tribe, being assured that they would do something for me. In view of these reasons they granted me, as I have said, four canoes, at which I was very happy, forgetting all past hardships in the hope of seeing this sea, as I so much desired.

For the remainder of the day, I went out walking in their gardens, which were filled with squashes, beans, and our peas, which they were beginning to cultivate, when Thomas, my interpreter, who understands the language very well, came to inform me that the savages, after I had left them, had come to the conclusion, that if I were to undertake this journey I should die and they also, and that they could not furnish the promised canoes, as there was no one of them who would guide me, but that they wished me to postpone the journey until the next year, when they would conduct me with a good train to protect me from that people, in case they should attempt to harm me, as they are evil-disposed.

This intelligence greatly disturbed me, and I at once went to them and told them, that up to this day I had regarded them as men and truthful persons, but that now they had shown themselves children and liars, and that if they would not fulfil their promises, they would fail to show me their friendship; that, however, if they felt it an inconvenience to give me four canoes they should only furnish two and four savages.

They represented to me anew the difficulties attending the journey, the number of the falls, the bad character of the people, and that their reason for refusing my request was their fear of losing me.

I replied that I was sorry to have them show themselves to so slight an extent my friends, and that I should never have believed it; that I had a young man, showing them my impostor, who had been in their country, and had not found all these difficulties which they represented, nor the people in question so bad as they asserted. Then they began to look at him, in particular Tessoüat the old captain, with whom he had passed the winter, and calling him by name he said to him in his language: Nicholas, is it true that you said you were among the Nebicerini? It was long before he spoke, when he said to them in their language, which he spoke to a certain extent: Yes, I was there. They immediately looked at him awry, and throwing themselves upon him, as if they would eat him up or tear him in pieces, raised loud cries, when Tessoüat said to him: You are a downright liar, you know well that you slept at my side every night with my children, where you arose every morning; if you were among the people mentioned, it was while sleeping. How could you have been so bold as to lead your chief to believe lies, and so wicked as to be willing to expose his life to so many dangers? You are a worthless fellow, and he ought to put you to death more cruelly than we do our enemies. I am not astonished that he should so importune us on the assurance of your words.

I at once told him that he must reply to these people; and since he had been in the regions indicated, that he must give me proofs of it, and free me from the suspense in which he had placed me. But he remained silent and greatly terrified.

I immediately withdrew him from the savages, and conjured him to declare the truth of the matter, telling him that, if he had seen the sea in question, I would give him the reward which I had promised him, and that, if he had not seen it, he must tell me so without causing me farther trouble. Again he affirmed with oaths all he had before said, and that he would demonstrate to me the truth of it, if the savages would give us canoes.

Upon this, Thomas came and informed me, that the savages of the island had secretly sent a canoe to the Nebicerini, to notify them of my arrival. Thereupon, in order to profit by the opportunity, I went to the savages to tell them, that I had dreamed the past night that they purposed to send a canoe to the Nebicerini without notifying me of it, at which I was greatly surprised, since they knew that I was desirous of going there. Upon which they replied that I did them a great wrong in trusting a liar, who wanted to cause my death, more than so many brave chiefs, who were my friends and who held my life dear. I replied that my man, meaning our impostor, had been in the aforesaid country with one of the relatives of Tessoüat and had seen the sea, the wreck and ruins of an English vessel, together with eighty scalps which the savages had in their possession, and a young English boy whom they held as prisoner, and whom they wished to give me as a present.

When they heard me speak of the sea, vessels, scalps of the English, and the young prisoner, they cried out more than before that he was a liar, and thus they afterwards called him, as if it were the greatest insult they could have done him, and they all united in saying that he ought to be put to death, or else that he should tell with whom he had gone to the place indicated, and state the lakes, rivers, and roads, by which he had gone. To this he replied with assurance, that he had forgotten the name of the savage, although he had stated to me his name more than twenty times, and even on the previous day. In respect to the peculiarities of the country, he had described them in a paper which he had handed me. Then I brought forward the map and had it explained to the savages, who questioned him in regard to it. To this he made no reply, but rather manifested by his sullen silence his perverse nature.

As my mind was wavering in uncertainty, I withdrew by myself, and reflected upon the above-mentioned particulars of the voyage of the English, and how the reports of our liar were quite in conformity with it, also that there was little probability of this young man's having invented all that, in which case he would not have been willing to undertake the journey, but that it was more probable that he had seen these things, and that his ignorance did not permit him to reply to the questions of the savages. To the above is to be added the fact that, if the report of the English be true, the North Sea cannot be farther distant from this region than a hundred leagues in latitude, for I was in latitude 47° and in longitude 296°.[71] But it may be that the difficulties attending the passage of the falls, the roughness of the mountains covered with shows, is the reason why this people have no knowledge of the sea in question; indeed they have always said that from the country of the Ochateguins it is a journey of thirty-five or forty days to the sea, which they see in three places, a thing which they have again assured me of this year. But no one has spoken to me of this sea on the north, except this liar, who had given me thereby great pleasure in view of the shortness of the journey.

Now, when this canoe was ready, I had him summoned into the presence of his companions; and after laying before him all that had transpired, I told him that any further dissimulation was out of the question, and that he must say whether he had seen these things or not; that I was desirous of improving the opportunity that presented itself; that I had forgotten the past; but that, if I went farther, I would have him hung and strangled, which should be his sole reward. After meditating by himself, he fell on his knees and asked my pardon, declaring that all he had said, both in France and this country, in respect to the sea in question was false; that he had never seen it, and that he had never gone farther than the village of Tessoüat; that he had said these things in order to return to Canada. Overcome with wrath at this, I had him removed, being unable to endure him any longer in my presence, and giving orders to Thomas to inquire into the whole matter in detail; to whom he stated, that he did not believe that I would undertake the journey on account of the dangers, thinking that some difficulty would present itself to prevent me from going on, as in the case of these savages, who were not disposed to lend me canoes; and accordingly that the journey would be put off until another year, when he being in France would be rewarded for his discovery; but that, if I would leave him in this country, he would go until he found the sea in question, even if he should die in the attempt. These were his words as reported to me by Thomas, but they did not give me much satisfaction, astounded as I was at the effrontery and maliciousness of this liar: and I cannot imagine how he could have devised this imposition, unless that he had heard of the above-mentioned voyage of the English, and in the hope of some reward, as he said, had the temerity to venture on it.

Shortly after I proceeded to notify the savages, to my great regret, of the malignity of this liar, stating that he had confessed the truth; at which they were delighted, reproaching me with the little confidence I put in them, who were chiefs and my friends, and who always spoke the truth; and who said that this liar ought to be put to death, being extremely malicious; and they added, Do you not see that he meant to cause your death. Give him to us, and we promise you that he shall not lie any more. And as they all went after him shouting, their children also shouting still more, I forbade them to do him any harm, directing them to keep their children also from doing so, inasmuch as I wished to take him to the Falls to show him to the gentlemen there, to whom he was to bring some salt water; and I said that, when I arrived there, I would consult as to what should be done with him.

My journey having been in this manner terminated, and without any hope of seeing the sea in this direction, except in imagination, I felt a regret that I should not have employed my time better, and that I should have had to endure the difficulties and hardships, which however I was obliged patiently to submit to. If I had gone in another direction, according to the report of the savages, I should have made a beginning in a thing which must be postponed to another time. At present my only wish being to return, I desired the savages to go to the Falls of St. Louis, where there were four vessels loaded with all kinds of merchandise, and where they would be well treated. This they communicated to all their neighbors. Before setting out, I made a cross of white cedar, which I planted in a prominent place on the border of the lake, with the arms of France, and I begged the savages to have the kindness to preserve it, as also those which they would find along the ways we had passed; telling them that, if they broke them, misfortune would befall them, but that, if they preserved them, they would not be assaulted by their enemies. They promised to do so, and said that I should find them when I came to visit them again.

ENDNOTES:

65. It seems not improbable, as suggested by Laverdière, that this was the same chief that Champlain met at Tadoussac in 1603, then called *Besouat. Vide* Vol. I. p. 242.

66. They crossed Muskrat Lake, and after a portage of a league, by general estimation, they reached Lake Allumette. This lake is only the expanded current of the river Ottawa on the southern side of Allumette Island; which is formed by the bifurcation of the Ottawa.

67. Allumette Island, often called, in the *Relations des Jésuites*, simply the Island. The savages in occupation were in the habit of exacting tribute from the Hurons and others, who passed along on their war excursions or their journeys for trade with the French at Montreal. They bartered their maize with other tribes for skins with which they clothed themselves.

68. The true latitude here is about 45° 47'. On the map of 1632 the latitude corresponds with the statement in the text.

69. In his issue of 1632 Champlain corrects his statement as to the length of Allumette Island, and says it is ten leagues long, which is nearly correct. *Vide* Quebec ed. p 868. Of this island Bouchette says that in length it is about fifteen miles, and on an average four miles wide.

British Dominions in North America, London, 1831, Vol I. p. 187.

70. This tribe was subsequently known as the Nipissings, who dwelt on the
borders of Lake Nipissing. They were distinguished for their sorceries,
under the cover of which they appear to have practised impositions
which naturally enough rendered other neighboring Algonquin tribes
hostile to them.

71. The true latitude, as we have stated, *antea*, note 61, is about 45° 37'; but on Champlain's map it corresponds with the statement in the text, and a hundred leagues north of where they then were, as his map is constructed, would carry them to the place in the bay where Hudson wintered, as stated by Champlain, and as laid down on his small map included in this volume; but the longitude is incorrect, Allumette Island being two or three degrees east of longitude 296°, as laid down on Champlain's map of 1632.

CHAPTER V.

OUR RETURN TO THE FALLS.—FALSE ALARM.—CEREMONY AT THE CHAUDIÈRE FALLS.— CONFESSION OF OUR LIAR BEFORE ALL THE CHIEF MEN.—OUR RETURN TO FRANCE.

On the 10th of June I took leave of Tessoüat, a good old captain, making him presents, and promising him, if God preserved me in health, to come the next year, prepared to go to war. He in turn promised to assemble a large number by that time, declaring that I should see nothing but savages and arms which would please me; he also directed his son to go with me for the sake of company. Thus we set out with forty canoes, and passed by way [72] of the river we had left, which extends northward, and where we went on shore in order to cross the lakes. On the way we met nine large canoes of the Ouescharini, with forty strong and powerful men, who had come upon the news they had received; we also met others, making all together sixty canoes; and we overtook twenty others, who had set out before us, each heavily laden with merchandise.

We passed six or seven falls between the island of the Algonquins [73] and the little fall, [74] where the country was very unpleasant I readily realized that, if we had gone in that direction, we should have had much more trouble, and would with difficulty have succeeded in getting through: and it was not without reason that the savages opposed our liar, as his only object was to cause my ruin.

Continuing our course ten or twelve leagues below the island of the Algonquins, we rested on a very pleasant island, which was covered with vines and nut-trees, and where we caught some fine fish. About midnight, there arrived two canoes, which had been fishing farther off, and which reported that they had seen four canoes of their enemies. At once three canoes were despatched to reconnoitre, but they returned without having seen anything. With this assurance all gave themselves up to sleep, excepting the women, who resolved to spend the night in their canoes, not feeling at ease on land. An hour before daylight a savage, having dreamed that the enemy were attacking them, jumped up and started on a run towards the water, in order to escape, shouting, They are killing me. Those belonging to his band all awoke dumfounded and, supposing that they were being pursued by their enemies, threw themselves into the water, as did also one of our Frenchmen, who supposed that they were being overpowered. At this great noise, the rest of us, who were at a distance, were at once awakened, and without making farther investigation ran towards them: but as we saw them here and there in the water, we were greatly surprised, not seeing them pursued by their enemies, nor in a state of defence, in case of necessity, but only ready to sacrifice themselves. After I had inquired of our Frenchman about the cause of this excitement, he told me that a savage had had a dream, and that he with the rest had thrown themselves into the water in order to escape, supposing that they were being attacked. Accordingly, the state of the case being ascertained, it all passed off in a laugh.

Continuing our way, we came to the Chaudière Falls, where the savages went through with the customary ceremony; which is as follows. After carrying their canoes to the foot of the Fall, they assemble in one spot, where one of them takes up a collection with a wooden plate, into which each one puts a bit of tobacco. The collection having been made, the plate is placed in the midst of the troupe, and all dance about it, singing after their style. Then one of the captains makes an harangue, setting forth that for a long time they have been accustomed to make this offering, by which means they are insured protection against their enemies, that otherwise misfortune would befall them, as they are convinced by the evil spirit; and they live on in this superstition, as in many others, as we have said in other places. This done, the maker of the harangue takes the plate, and throws the tobacco into the midst of the caldron, whereupon they all together raise a loud cry. These poor people are so superstitious, that they would not believe it possible for them to make a prosperous journey without observing this ceremony at this place, since their enemies await them at this portage, not venturing to go any farther on account of the difficulty of the journey, whence they say they surprise them there, as they have sometimes done.

The next day we arrived at an island at the entrance to a lake, and seven or eight leagues distant from the great Falls of St. Louis. Here while reposing at night we had another alarm, the savages supposing that they had seen the canoes of their enemies. This led them to make several large fires, which I had them put out, representing to them the harm which might result, namely, that instead of concealing they would disclose themselves.

On the 17th of June, we arrived at the Falls of St. Louis, where I found L'Ange, who had come to meet me in a canoe to inform me, that Sieur de Maisonneuve of St. Malo had brought a passport from the Prince for three vessels. In order to arrange matters until I should see him, I assembled all the savages and informed them that I did not wish them to traffic in any merchandise until I had given them permission, and that I would furnish them provisions as soon as we should arrive; which they promised, saying that they were my friends. Thus, continuing our course, we arrived at the barques, where we were saluted by some discharges of cannon, at which some of our savages were delighted, and others greatly astonished, never having heard such music. After I had landed, Maisonneuve came to me with the passport of the Prince. As soon as I had seen it, I allowed him and his men to enjoy the benefits of it like the rest of us; and I sent word to the savages that they might trade on the next day.

After seeing all the chief men and relating the particulars of my journey and the malice of my liar, at which they were greatly amazed, I begged them to assemble, in order that in their presence, and that of the savages and his companions, he might make declaration of his maliciousness; which they gladly did. Being thus assembled, they summoned him, and asked him, why he had not shown me the sea in the north, as he had promised me at his departure. He replied that he had promised something impossible for him, since he had never seen this sea, and that the desire of making the journey had led him to say what he did, also that he did not suppose that I would undertake it; and he begged them to be pleased to pardon him, as he also did me again, confessing that he had greatly offended, and if I would leave him in the country, he would by his efforts repair the offence, and see this sea, and bring back trustworthy intelligence concerning it the following year; and in view of certain considerations I pardoned him on this condition.

After relating to them in detail the good treatment I had received at the abodes of the savages, and how I had been occupied each day, I inquired what they had done during my absence, and what had been the result of their hunting excursions, and they said they had had such success that they generally brought home six stags. Once on St. Barnabas's day, Sieur du Parc, having gone hunting with two others, killed nine. These stags are not at all like ours, and there are different kinds of them, some larger, others smaller, which resemble closely our deer.[75] They had also a very large number of pigeons, [76] and also fish, such as pike, carp, sturgeon, shad, barbel, turtles, bass, and other kinds unknown to us, on which they dined and supped every day. They were also all in better condition than myself, who was reduced from work and the anxiety which I had experienced, not having eaten more than once a day, and that of fish badly cooked and half broiled.

On the 22d of June, about 8 o'clock in the evening, the savages sounded an alarm because one of them had dreamed he had seen the Iroquois. In order to content them, all the men took their arms, and some were sent to their cabins to reassure them, and into the approaches to reconnoitre, so that, finding it was a false alarm, they were satisfied with the firing of some two hundred musket and arquebus shots, after which arms were laid down, the ordinary guard only being left. This reassured them greatly, and they were very glad to see the French ready to help them.

After the savages had bartered their articles of merchandise and had resolved to return, I asked them to take with them two young men, to treat them in a friendly manner, show them the country, and bind themselves to bring them back. But they strongly objected to this, representing to me the trouble our liar had given me, and fearing that they would bring me false reports, as he had done. I replied that they were men of probity and truth, and that if they would not take them they were not my friends, whereupon they resolved to do so. As for out liar, none of the savages wanted him, notwithstanding my request to them to take him, and we left him to the mercy of God.

Finding that I had no further, business in this country, I resolved to cross in the first vessel that should return to France. Sieur de Maisonneuve, having his ready, offered me a passage, which I accepted; and on the 27th of June I set out with Sieur L'Ange from the Falls, where we left the other vessels, which were awaiting the return of the savages who had gone to the war, and we arrived at Tadoussac on the 6th of July.

On the 8th of August [77] we were enabled by favorable weather to set sail. On the 18th we left Gaspé and Isle Percée. On the 28th we were on the Grand Bank, where the green fishery is carried on, and where we took as many fish as we wanted.

On the 26th of August we arrived at St Malo, where I saw the merchants, to whom I represented the ease of forming a good association in the future, which they resolved to do, as those of Rouen and La Rochelle had done, after recognizing the necessity of the regulations, without which it is impossible to hope for any profit from these lands. May God by His grace cause this undertaking to prosper to His honor and glory, the conversion of these poor benighted ones, and to the welfare and honor of France.

ENDNOTES:

72. By the Ottawa, which they had left a little below Portage du Fort, and not by the same way they had come, through the system of small lakes, of which Muskrat lake is one. *Vide Carte de la Nouvelle France*, 1632, Vol. I. p. 304.

73. Allumette Island.

74. Near Gould's Landing, below or south of Portage da Fort. — *Vide Champlain's Astrolabe*, by A. J. Russell, Montreal, 1879, p. 6.

75. At that time there were to be found in Canada at least four species of
the Cervus Family.

1. The Moose, *Cervus alces*, or *alces Americanus*, usually called by the earliest writers *orignal* or *orignac*. *Vide* Vol. I. pp. 264, 265. This is the largest of all the deer

family in this or in any other part of the world The average weight has been placed at seven hundred pounds, while extraordinary specimens probably attain twice that weight.

2. The Wapiti, or American Elk, *Cervus elaphus*, or *Canadensis*. This is the largest of the known deer except the preceding. The average weight is probably less than six hundred pounds.

3. The Woodland Caribou, *Cervus tarandus*. It is smaller than the Wapiti. Its range is now mostly in the northern regions of the continent but specimens are still found in Nova Scotia and New Brunswick. The female is armed with antlers as well as the male, though they are smaller.

4. The Common Deer, *Cervus Virginianus*. It has the widest range of any of the deer family. It is still found in every degree of latitude from Mexico to British Columbia. *Vide Antelope and Deer of America* by John Dean Caton, LL.D., Boston, 1877.

76. *Palombes*. The passenger, or wild pigeon, *Ectopistes migratorius*.

77. *Le* 8 *Aoust*. Laverdière suggests with much plausibility that this should read "The 8th of July." Champlain could hardly have found it necessary to remain at Tadoussac from the 6th of July to the 8th of August for favorable weather to sail. If he had been detained by any other cause, it would probably nave been deemed of sufficient gravity to be specially mentioned.

VOYAGES
AND
DISCOVERIES IN NEW FRANCE,
From the year 1615 to the end of the year 1618.

BY
SIEUR DE CHAMPLAIN,

Captain in ordinary to the King in the Western Sea.

WHERE ARE DESCRIBED

_The manners, customs, dress, mode of warfare, hunting, dances, festivals, and method of burial of various savage peoples, with many remarkable experiences of the author in this country, and an account of the beauty, fertility, and temperature of the same.

PARIS.

CLAUDE COLLET, in the Palace, at the gallery of the Prisoners.

M. DC. XIX.

WITH AUTHORITY OF THE KING.

TO THE KING.

Sire, This is a third volume containing a narrative of what has transpired most worthy of note during the voyages I have made to New France, and its perusal will, I think, afford your Majesty greater pleasure than that of those preceding, which only designate the ports, harbors, situations, declinations, and other particulars, having more interest for navigators and sailors than for other persons. In this narrative you will be able to observe more especially the manners and mode of life of these peoples both in particular and in general, their wars, ammunition, method of attack and of defence, their expeditions and retreats in various circumstances, matters about which those interested desire information. You will perceive also that they are not savage to such an extent that they could not in course of time and through association with others become civilised and cultivated. You will likewise perceive how great hopes we cherish from the long and arduous labors we have for the past fifteen years sustained, in order to plant in this country the standard of the cross, and to teach the people the knowledge of God and the glory of His holy name, it being our desire to cultivate a feeling of charity towards His unfortunate creatures, which it is our duty to practise more patiently than any other thing, especially as there are many who have not entertained such purposes, but have been influenced only by the desire of gain. Nevertheless we may, I suppose, believe that these are the means which God makes use of for the greater promotion of the holy desire of others. As the fruits which the trees bear are from God, the Lord of the soil, who has planted, watered, and nourished them with an especial care, so your Majesty can be called the legitimate lord of our labors, and the good resulting from them, not only because the land belongs to you, but also because you have protected us against so many persons, whose only object has been by troubling us to prevent the success of so holy a determination, taking from us the power to trade freely in apart of your country, and striving to bring everything into confusion, which would be, in a word, preparing the way for the ruin of everything to the injury of your state. To this end your subjects have employed every conceivable artifice and all possible means which they thought could injure us. But all these efforts have been thwarted by your Majesty, assisted by your prudent council, who have given us the authority of your name, and supported us by your decrees rendered in our favor. This is an occasion for increasing in us our long-cherished desire to send communities and colonies there, to teach the people the knowledge of God, and inform them of the glory and triumphs of your Majesty, so that together with the French language they may also acquire a French heart and spirit, which, next to the fear of God, will be inspired with nothing so ardently as the desire to serve you. Should our design succeed, the glory of it will be due, after God, to your Majesty, who will receive a thousand benedictions from Heaven for so many souls saved by your instrumentality, and your name will be immortalized for carrying the glory and sceptre of the French as far to the Occident as your precursors have extended it to the Orient, and over the entire habitable earth. This will augment the quality of MOST CHRISTIAN *belonging to you above all the kings of the earth, and show that it is as much your due by merit as it is your own of right, it having been transmitted to you by your predecessors, who acquired it by their virtues; for you have been pleased, in addition to so many other important affairs, to give your attention to this one, so seriously neglected hitherto, God's special grace reserving to your reign the publication of His gospel, and the knowledge of His holy name to so many tribes who had never heard of it. And some day may God's grace lead them, as it does us, to pray to Him without ceasing to extend your empire, and to vouchsafe a thousand blessings to your Majesty.*

SIRE,

Your most humble, most faithful,

and most obedient servant and subject,

CHAMPLAIN.

PREFACE.

As in the various affairs of the world each thing strives for its perfection and the preservation of its being, so on the other hand does man interest himself in the different concerns of others on some account, either for the public good, or to acquire, apart from the common interest, praise and reputation with some profit. Wherefore many have pursued this course, but as for myself I have made choice of the most unpleasant and difficult one of the perilous navigation of the seas; with the purpose, however, not so much of gaining wealth, as the honor and glory of God in behalf of my King and country, and contributing by my labors something useful to the public good. And I make declaration that I have not been tempted by any other ambition, as can be clearly perceived, not only by my conduct in the past, but also by the narratives of my voyages, made by the command of His Majesty, in New France, contained in my first and second books, as may be seen in the same.

Should God bless our purpose, which aims only for His glory, and should any fruit result from our discoveries and arduous labors, I will return thanks to Him, and for Your Majesty's protection and assistance will continue my prayers for the aggrandizement and prolongation of your reign.

EXTRACT FROM THE LICENSE OF THE KING.

By favor and license of the KING, permission is given to CLAUDE COLLET, merchant bookseller in our city of Paris, to print, or have printed by such printer as shall seem good to him, a book entitled, *Voyages and Discoveries in New France, from the Year* 1615 *to the End of the Year 1618. By Sieur de Champlain, Captain in Ordinary to the King in the Western Sea.* All booksellers and printers of our kingdom are forbidden to print or have printed, to sell wholesale or retail, said book, except with the consent of said Collet, for the time and term of six years, beginning with the day when said book is printed, on penalty of confiscation of the copies, and a fine of four hundred *livres*, a half to go to us and a half to said petitioner. It is our will, moreover, that this License should be placed at the commencement or end of said book. This is our pleasure.

Given at Paris, the 18th day of May, 1619, and of our reign the tenth.

By the Council,

DE CESCAUD

VOYAGE OF SIEUR DE CHAMPLAIN TO NEW FRANCE, MADE IN THE YEAR 1615.

The strong love, which I have always cherished for the exploration of New France, has made me desirous of extending more and more my travels over the country, in order, by means of its numerous rivers, lakes, and streams, to obtain at last a complete knowledge of it, and also to become acquainted with the inhabitants, with the view of bringing them to the knowledge of God. To this end I have toiled constantly for the past fourteen or fifteen years, [78] yet have been able to advance my designs but little, because I have not received the assistance which was necessary for the success of such an undertaking. Nevertheless, without losing courage, I have not ceased to push on, and visit various nations of the savages; and, by associating familiarly with them, I have concluded, as well from their conversation as from the knowledge already attained, that there is no better way than, disregarding all storms and difficulties, to have patience until His Majesty shall give the requisite attention to the matter, and meanwhile, not only to continue the exploration of the country, but also to learn the language, and form relations and friendships with the leading men of the villages and tribes, in order to lay the foundations of a permanent edifice, as well for the glory of God as for the renown of the French.

And His Majesty having transferred and intrusted the superintendence of this work to Monseigneur the Prince de Condé, the latter has, by his management, under the authority of His Majesty, sustained us against all forts of jealousies and obstacles concerted by evil wishers. This has, as it were, animated me and redoubled my courage for the continuation of my labors in the exploration of New France, and with increased effort I have pushed forward in my undertaking into the mainland, and farther on than I had previously been, as will be hereafter indicated in the course of this narrative.

But it is appropriate to state first that, as I had observed in my previous journeys, there were in some places people permanently settled, who were fond of the cultivation of the soil, but who had neither faith nor law, and lived without God and religion, like brute beasts. In view of this, I felt convinced that I should be committing a grave offence if I did not take it upon myself to devise some means of bringing them to the knowledge of God. To this end I exerted myself to find some good friars, with zeal and affection for the glory of God, that I might persuade them to send some one, or go themselves, with me to these countries, and try to plant there the faith, or at least do what was possible according to their calling, and thus to observe and ascertain whether any good fruit could be gathered there. But since to attain this object an expenditure would be required exceeding my means, and for other reasons, I deferred the matter for a while, in view of the difficulties there would be in obtaining what was necessary and requisite in such an enterprise; and since, furthermore, no persons offered to contribute to it. Nevertheless, while continuing my search, and communicating my plan to various persons, a man of distinction chanced to present himself, whose intimate acquaintance I enjoyed. This was Sieur Hoüel, Secretary of the King and Controller-general of the salt works at Brouage, a man of devoted piety, and of great zeal and love for the honor of God and the extension of His religion. [79] He gave me the following information, which afforded me great pleasure. He said that he was acquainted with some good religious Fathers, of the order of the Recollects, in whom he had confidence; and that he enjoyed such intimacy and confidence with them that he could easily induce them to consent to undertake the voyage; and that, as to the necessary means for sending out three or four friars, there would be no lack of people of property who would give them what they needed, offering for his part to assist them to the extent of his ability; and, in fact, he wrote in relation to the subject to Father du Verger, [80] who welcomed with joy the undertaking, and, in accordance with the recommendation of Sieur Hoüel, communicated it to some of his brethren, who, burning with charity, offered themselves freely for this holy undertaking.

Now he was at that time in Saintonge, whence he sent two men to Paris with a commission, though not with absolute power, reserving the rest to the Nuncio of our Holy Father the Pope, who was at that time, in 1614, in France. [81] He called upon these friars at their house in Paris, and was greatly pleased with their resolution. We then went all together to see the Sieur Nuncio, in order to communicate to him the commission, and entreat him to interpose his authority in the matter. But he, on the contrary, told us that he had no power whatever in such matters, and that it was to their General that they were to address themselves. Notwithstanding this reply, the Recollects, in consideration of the difficulty of the mission, were unwilling to undertake the journey on the authority of Father du Verger, fearing that it might not be sufficient, and that the commission might not be valid, on which account the matter was postponed to the following year. Meanwhile they took counsel, and came to a determination, according to which all arrangements were made for the undertaking, which was to be carried out in the following spring; awaiting which the two friars returned to their convent at Brouage.

I for my part improved the time in arranging my affairs in preparation for the voyage.

Some months after the departure of the two friars, the Reverend Father Chapoüin, Provincial of the Recollect Fathers, a man of great piety, returned to Paris. Sieur, Hoüel called on him, and narrated what had taken place respecting the authority of Father du Verger, and the mission he had given to the Recollect Fathers. After which narrative the Provincial Father proceeded to extol the plan, and to interest himself with zeal in it, promising to promote it with all his power, and adding that, he had not before well comprehended the subject of this mission; and it is to be believed that God inspired him more and more to prosecute the matter. Subsequently he spoke of it to Monseigneur the Prince de Condé, and to all the cardinals and bishops who were then assembled at Paris for the Session of the Estates. All of them approved and commended the plan; and to show that they were favorably disposed towards it, they assured the Sieur Provincial that they would devise among themselves and the members of the Court means for raising a small fund, and that they would collect some money for assisting four friars to be chosen, and who were then chosen for the execution of so holy a work. And in order to facilitate the undertaking, I visited at the Estates the cardinals and bishops, and urgently represented to them the advantage, and usefulness which might one day result, in order by my entreaties to move them to give, and cause others who might be stimulated by their example to give, contributions and presents, leaving all to their good will and judgment.

The contributions which were made for the expenses of this expedition amounted to nearly fifteen hundred *livres*, which were put into my hands, and then employed, according to the advice and in the presence of the Fathers, for the purchase of what was necessary, not only for the maintenance of the Fathers who should undertake the journey into New France, but also for their clothing, and the attire and ornaments necessary for performing divine service. The friars were sent on in advance to Honfleur, where their embarkation was to take place.

Now the Fathers who were appointed for this holy enterprise were Father Denis [82] as commissary, Jean d'Olbeau, [83] Joseph le Caron, and Pacifique du Plessis, [84] each of whom was moved by a holy zeal and ardor to make the journey, through God's grace, in order to see if they might produce some good fruit, and plant in these regions the standard of Jesus Christ, determined to live and to die for His holy name, should it be necessary to do so and the occasion require it. Everything having been prepared, they provided themselves with church ornaments, and we with what was necessary for our voyage.

I left Paris the last day of February to meet at Rouen our associates, and represent to them the will of Monseigneur the Prince, and also his desire that these good Fathers should make the journey, since he recognized the fact that the affairs of the country could hardly reach any perfection or advancement, if God should not first of all be served; with which our associates were highly pleased, promising to assist the Fathers to the extent of their ability, and provide them with the support they might need.

The Fathers arrived at Rouen the twentieth of March following, where we stayed some time. Thence we went to Honfleur to embark, where we also stayed some days, waiting for our vessel to be got ready, and loaded with the necessaries for so long a voyage. Meanwhile preparations were made in matters of conscience, so that each one of us might examine himself, and cleanse himself from his sins by penitence and confession, in order to celebrate the sacrament and attain a state of grace, so that, being thereby freer in conscience, we might under the guidance of God, expose ourselves to the mercy of the waves of the great and perilous sea.

This done, we embarked on the vessel of the association, which was of three hundred and fifty tons burden, and was called the Saint Étienne, commanded by Sieur de Pont Gravé. We departed from Honfleur on the twenty-fourth day of August, [85] in the above-mentioned year, and set sail with a very favorable wind. We continued on our voyage without encountering ice or other dangers, through the mercy of God, and in a short time arrived off the place called *Tadoussac*, on the twenty-fifth day of May, when we rendered thanks to God for having conducted us so favorably to the harbor of our destination.

Then we began to set men at work to fit up our barques in order to go to Quebec, the place of our abode, and to the great Falls of Saint Louis, the rendezvous of the savages, who come there to traffic.

The barques having been fitted up, we went on board with the Fathers, one of whom, named Father Joseph, [86] desired, without stopping or making any stay at Quebec, to go directly to the great Falls, where he saw all the savages and their mode of life. This induced him to go and spend the winter in their country and that of other tribes who have a fixed abode, not only in order to learn their language, but also to see what the prospect was of their conversion to Christianity. This resolution having been formed, he returned to Quebec the twentieth day of June [87] for some church ornaments and other necessaries. Meanwhile I had stayed at Quebec in order to arrange matters relating to our habitation, as the lodgings of the Fathers, church ornaments, the construction of a chapel for the celebration of the mass, as also the employment of persons for clearing up lands. I embarked for the Falls together with Father Denis, [88] who had arrived the same day from Tadoussac with Sieur de Pont Gravé.

As to the other friars, viz., Fathers Jean and Pacifique, [89] they stayed at Quebec in order to fit up their chapel and arrange their lodgings. They were greatly pleased at seeing the place so different from what they had imagined, which increased their zeal.

We arrived at the Rivière des Prairies, five leagues below the Falls of Saint Louis, whither the savages had come down. I will not attempt to speak of the pleasure which our Fathers experienced at seeing, not only so long and large a river, filled with many fine islands and bordered by a region apparently so fertile, but also a great number of strong and robust men, with natures not so savage as their manners, nor as they acknowledged they had conceived them to be, and very different from what they had been given to understand, owing to their lack of cultivation. I will not enter into a description of them, but refer the reader to what I have said about them in my preceding books, printed in the year 1614. [90]

To continue my narrative: We met Father Joseph, who was returning to Quebec in order to make preparations, and take what he needed for wintering in their country. This I did not think advisable at this season, but counselled him rather to spend the winter at our settlement as being more for his comfort, and undertake the journey when spring came or at least in summer, offering to accompany him, and adding that by doing so he would not fail to see what he might have seen by going, and that by returning and spending the winter at Quebec he would have the society of his brothers and others who remained at the settlement, by which he would be more profited than by staying alone among these people, with whom he could not, in my opinion, have much satisfaction. Nevertheless, in spite of all that could be said to him and all representations, he would not change his purpose, being urged by a godly zeal and love for this people, and hoping to make known to them their salvation.

His motive in undertaking this enterprise, as he stated to us, was that he thought it was necessary for him to go there not only in order to become better acquainted with the characteristics of the people, but also to learn more easily their language. In regard to the difficulties which it was represented to him that he would have to encounter in his intercourse with them, he felt assured that he could bear and overcome them, and that he could adapt himself very well and cheerfully to the manner of living and the inconveniences he would find, through the grace of God, of whose goodness and help he felt clearly assured, being convinced that, since he went on His service, and since it was for the glory of His name and the preaching of His holy gospel that he undertook freely this journey, He would never abandon him in his undertaking. And in regard to temporal provisions very little was needed to satisfy a man who demands nothing but perpetual poverty, and who seeks for nothing but heaven, not only for himself but also for his brethren, it not being consistent with his rule of life to have any other ambition than the glory of God, and it being his purpose to endure to this end all the hardships, sufferings, and labors which might offer.

Seeing him impelled by so holy a zeal and so ardent a charity, I was unwilling to try any more to restrain him. Thus he set out with the purpose of being the first to announce through His holy favor to this people the name of God, having the great satisfaction that an opportunity presented itself for suffering something for the name and glory of our Saviour Jesus Christ.

As soon as I had arrived at the Falls, I visited the people, who were very desirous of seeing us and delighted at our return. They hoped that we would furnish them some of our number to assist them in their wars against our enemies, representing to us that they could with difficulty come to us if we should not assist them; for the Iroquois, they said, their old enemies, were always on the road obstructing their passage. Moreover I had constantly promised to assist them in their wars, as they gave us to understand by their interpreter. Whereupon Sieur Pont Gravé and myself concluded that it was very necessary to assist them, not only in order to put them the more under obligations to love us, but also to facilitate my undertakings and explorations which, as it seemed, could only be accomplished by their help, and also as this would be a preparatory step to their conversion to Christianity. [91] Therefore I resolved to, go and explore their country and assist them in their wars, in order to oblige them to show me what they had so many times promised to do.

We accordingly caused them all to assemble together, that we might communicate to them our intention. When they had heard it, they promised to furnish us two thousand five hundred and fifty men of war, who would do wonders, with the understanding that I with the same end in view should very glad to see them decide so well. Then I proceeded to make known to them the methods to be adopted for fighting, in which they took especial pleasure, manifesting a strong hope of victory. Everything having been decided upon, we separated with the intention of returning for the execution of our undertaking. But before entering upon this journey, which would require not less than three or four months, it seemed desirable that I should go to our settlement to make the necessary arrangements there for my absence.

On the –– day of –– following I set out on my return to the Rivière des Prairies. [92] While there with two canoes of savages I met Father Joseph, who was returning from our settlement with some church ornaments for celebrating the holy sacrifice of the mass, which was chanted on the border of the river with all devotion by the Reverend Fathers Denis and Joseph, in presence of all the people, who were amazed at seeing the ceremonies observed and the ornaments which seemed to them so handsome. It was something which they had never before seen, for these Fathers were the first who celebrated here the holy mass.

To return and continue the narrative of my journey: I arrived at Quebec on the 26th, where I found the Fathers Jean and Pacifique in good health. They on their part did their duty at that place in getting all things ready. They celebrated the holy mass, which had never been said there before, nor had there ever been any priest in this region.

Having arranged all matters at Quebec, I took with me two men and returned to the Rivière des Prairies, in order to go with the savages. I left Quebec on the fourth day of July, and on the eighth of the month while *en route* I met Sieur du Pont Gravé and Father Denis, who were returning to Quebec, and who told me that the savages had departed greatly disappointed at my not going with them; and that many of them declared that we were dead or had been taken by the Iroquois, since I was to be gone only four or five days, but had been gone ten. This made them and even our own Frenchmen give up hope, so much did they long to see us again. They told me that Father Joseph had departed with twelve Frenchmen, who had been furnished to assist the savages. This intelligence troubled me somewhat; since, if I had been there, I should have arranged many things for the journey, which I could not now do. I was troubled not only on account of the small number of men, but also because there were only four or five who were acquainted with the handling of arms, while in such an expedition the best are not too good in this particular. All this however did not cause me to lose courage at all for going on with the expedition, on account of the desire I had of continuing my explorations. I separated accordingly from Sieurs du Pont Gravé and Father Denis, determined to go on in the two canoes which I had, and follow after the savages, having provided myself with what I needed.

On the 9th of the month I embarked with two others, namely, one of our interpreters [93] and my man, accompanied by ten savages in the two canoes, these being all they could carry, as they were heavily loaded and encumbered with clothes, which prevented me from taking more men.

We continued our voyage up the River St. Lawrence some six leagues, and then went by the Rivière des Prairies, which discharges into that river. Leaving on the left the Falls of St. Louis, which are five or six leagues higher up, and passing several small falls on this river, we entered a lake, [94] after passing which we entered the river where I had been before, which leads to the Algonquins, [95] a distance of eighty-nine leagues [96] from the Falls of St. Louis. Of this river I have made an ample description, with an account of my explorations, in my preceding book, printed in 1614.[97] For this reason I shall not speak of it in this narrative, but pass on directly to the lake of the Algonquins.[98] Here we entered a river [99] which flows into this lake, up which we went some thirty-five leagues, passing a large number of falls both by land and water, the country being far from attractive, and covered with pines, birches, and some oaks, being also very rocky, and in many places somewhat hilly. Moreover it was very barren and sterile, being but thinly inhabited by certain Algonquin savages, called *Otaguottouemin*, [100] who dwell in the country, and live by hunting and the fish they catch in the rivers, ponds, and lakes, with which the region is well provided. It seems indeed that God has been pleased to give to these forbidding and desert lands some things in their season for the refreshment of man and the inhabitants of these places. For I assure you that there are along the rivers many strawberries, also a marvellous quantity of blueberries, [101] a little fruit very good to eat, and other small fruits. The people here dry these fruits for the winter, as we do plums in France for Lent We left this river, which comes from the north, [102] and by which the savages go to the Saguenay to barter their furs for tobacco. This place is situated in latitude 46°, and is very pleasant, but otherwise of little account. [103]

Continuing our journey by land, after leaving the river of the Algonquins, we passed several lakes [104] where the savages carry their canoes, and entered the lake of the Nipissings,[105] in latitude 46° 15', on the twenty-sixth day of the month, having gone by land and the lakes twenty- five leagues, or thereabouts.[106] We then arrived at the cabins of the savages, with whom we stayed two days. There was a large number of them, who gave us a very welcome reception. They are a people who cultivate the land but little. A shows the dress of these people as they go to war; B that of the women, which differs in no wise from that of the Montagnais and the great people of the Algonquins, extending far into the interior.[107]

During the time that I was with them the chief of this tribe and their most prominent men entertained us with many banquets according to their custom, and took the trouble to go fishing and hunting with me, in order to treat me with the greatest courtesy possible. These people are very numerous, there being from seven to eight hundred souls, who live in general near the lake. This contains a large number of very pleasant islands, among others one more than six leagues long, with three or four fine ponds and a number of fine meadows; it is bordered by very fine woods, that contain an abundance of game, which frequent the little ponds, where the savages also catch fish. The northern side of the lake is very pleasant, with fine meadows for the grazing of cattle, and many little streams, discharging into the lake.

They were fishing at that time in a lake very abundant in various kinds of fish, among others one a foot long that was very good. There are also other kinds which the savages catch for the purpose of drying and storing away. The lake is some eight leagues broad and twenty-five long,[108] into which a river [109] flows from the northwest, along which they go to barter the merchandise, which we give them in exchange for their peltry, with, those who live on it, and who support themselves by hunting and fishing, their country containing great quantities of animals, birds, and fish.[110]

After resting two days with the chief of the Nipissings we re-embarked in our canoes, and entered a river, by which this lake discharges itself.[111] We proceeded down it some thirty-five leagues, and descended several little falls by land and by water, until we reached Lake Attigouautan. All this region is still more unattractive than the preceding, for I saw along this river only ten acres of arable land, the rest being rocky and very hilly. It is true that near Lake Attigouautan we found some Indian corn, but only in small quantity. Here our savages proceeded to gather some squashes, which were acceptable to us, for our provisions began to give out in consequence of the bad management of the savages, who ate so heartily at the beginning that towards the end very little was left, although we had only one meal a day. But, as I have mentioned before, we did not lack for blueberries [112] and strawberries; otherwise we should have been in danger of being reduced to straits.

We met three hundred men of a tribe we named *Cheveux Relevés,* [113] since their hair is very high and carefully arranged, and better dressed beyond all comparison than that of our courtiers, in spite of their irons and refinements. This gives them a handsome appearance. They have no breeches, and their bodies are very much pinked in divisions of various shapes. They paint their faces in various colors, have their nostrils pierced, and their ears adorned with beads. When they go out of their houses they carry a club. I visited them, became somewhat acquainted, and formed a friendship with them. I gave a hatchet to their chief, who was as much pleased and delighted with it as if I had given him some rich present. Entering into conversation with him, I inquired in regard to the extent of his country, which he pictured to me with coal on the bark of a tree. He gave me to understand that he had come into this place for drying the fruit called *bluës* [114] to serve for manna in winter, and when they can find nothing else. A and C show the manner in which they arm themselves when they go to war. They have as arms only the bow and arrow, made in the manner you see depicted, and which they regularly carry; also a round shield of dressed leather [115] made from an animal like the buffalo. [116]

The next day we separated, and continued our course, along the shore of the lake of the Attigouautan, [117] which contains a large number of islands. We went some forty-five leagues, all the time along the shore of the lake. It is very large, nearly four hundred leagues long from east to west, and fifty leagues broad, and in view of its great extent I have named it the *Mer Douce*. [118] It is very abundant in various sorts of very good fish, both those which we have and those we do not, but especially in trout, which are enormously large, some of which I saw as long as four feet and a half, the least being two feet and a half. There are also pike of like size, and a certain kind of sturgeon, a very large fish and of remarkable excellence. The country bordering this lake is partly hilly, as on the north side, and partly flat, inhabited by savages, and thinly covered with wood, including oaks. After crossing a bay, which forms one of the extremities of the lake, [119] we went some seven leagues until we arrived in the country of the Attigouautan at a village called *Otoüacha*, on the first day of August. Here we found a great change in the country. It was here very fine, the largest part being cleared up, and many hills and several rivers rendering the region agreeable. I went to see their Indian corn, which was at that time far advanced for the season.

These localities seemed to me very pleasant, in comparison with so disagreeable a region as that from which we had come. The next day I went to another village, called *Carmaron*, a league distant from this, where they received us in a very friendly manner, making for us a banquet with their bread, squashes, and fish. As to meat, that is very scarce there. The chief of this village earnestly begged me to stay, to which I could not consent, but returned to our village, where on the next night but one, as I went out of the cabin to escape the fleas, of which there were large numbers and by which we were tormented, a girl of little modesty came boldly to me and offered to keep me company, for which I thanked her, sending her away with gentle remonstrances, and spent the night with some savages.

The next day I departed from this village to go to another, called *Touaguainchain*, and to another, called *Tequenonquiaye*, in which we were received in a very friendly manner by the inhabitants, who showed us the best cheer they could with their Indian corn served in various styles. This country is very fine and fertile, and travelling through it is very pleasant.

Thence I had them guide me to Carhagouha, which was fortified by a triple palisade of wood thirty-five feet high for its defence and protection. In this village Father Joseph was staying, whom we saw and were very glad to find well. He on his part was no less glad, and was expecting nothing so little as to see me in this country. On the twelfth day of August the Recollect Father celebrated the holy mass, and a cross was planted near a small house apart from the village, which the savages built while I was staying there, awaiting the arrival of our men and their preparation to go to the war, in which they had been for a long time engaged.

Finding that they were so slow in assembling their army, and that I should have time to visit their country, I resolved to go by short days' journeys from village to village as far as Cahiagué, where the rendezvous of the entire army was to be, and which was fourteen leagues distant from Carhagouha, from which village I set out on the fourteenth of August with ten of my companions. I visited five of the more important villages, which were enclosed with palisades of wood, and reached Cahiagué, the principal village of the country, where there were two hundred large cabins and where all the men of war were to assemble. Now in all these villages they received us very courteously with their simple welcome. All the country where I went contains some twenty to thirty leagues, is very fine, and situated in latitude 44° 30'. It is very extensively cleared up. They plant in it a great quantity of Indian corn, which grows there finely. They plant likewise squashes,[120] and sun-flowers,[121] from the seed of which they make oil, with which they anoint the head. The region is extensively traversed with brooks, discharging into the lake. There are many very good vines [122] and plums, which are excellent,[123] raspberries,[124] strawberries,[125] little wild apples,[126] nuts,[127] and a kind of fruit of the form and color of small lemons, with a similar taste, but having an interior which is very good and almost like that of figs. The plant which bears this fruit is two and a half feet high, with but three or four leaves at most, which are of the shape of those of the fig-tree, and each plant bears but two pieces of fruit. There are many of these plants in various places, the fruit being very good and savory.[128] Oaks, elms, and beeches [129] are numerous here, as also forests of fir, the regular retreat of partridges [130] and hares.[131] There are also quantities of small cherries [132] and black cherries,[133] and the same varieties of wood that we have in our forests in France. The soil seems to me indeed a little sandy, yet it is for all that good for their kind of cereal. The small tract of country which I visited is thickly settled with a countless number of human beings, not to speak of the other districts where I did not go, and which, according to general report, are as thickly settled or more so than those mentioned above. I reflected what a great misfortune it is that so many poor creatures live and die without the knowledge of God, and even without any religion or law established among them, whether divine, political, or civil; for they neither worship, nor pray to any object, at least so far as I could perceive from their conversation. But they have, however, some sort of ceremony, which I shall describe in its proper place, in regard to the sick, or in order to ascertain what is to happen to them, and even in regard to the dead. These, however, are the works of certain persons among them, who want to be confidentially consulted in such matters, as was the case among the ancient pagans, who allowed themselves to be carried away by the persuasions of magicians and diviners. Yet the greater part of the people do not believe at all in what these charlatans do and say. They are very generous to one another in regard to provisions, but otherwise very avaricious. They do not give in return. They are clothed with deer and beaver skins, which they obtain from the Algonquins and Nipissings in exchange for Indian corn and meal.

On the 17th of August I arrived at Cahiagué, where I was received with great joy and gladness by all the savages of the country, who had abandoned their undertaking, in the belief that they would see me no more, and that the Iroquois had captured me, as I have before stated. This was the cause of the great delay experienced in this expedition, they even having postponed it to the following year. Meanwhile they received intelligence that a certain nation of their allies, [134] dwelling three good days' journeys beyond the Entouhonorons, [135] on whom the Iroquois also make war, desired to assist them in this expedition with five hundred good men; also to form an alliance and establish a friendship with us, that we might all engage in the war together; moreover that they greatly desired to see us and give expression to the pleasure they would have in making our acquaintance.

I was glad to find this opportunity for gratifying my desire of obtaining a knowledge of their country. It is situated only seven days from where the Dutch [136] go to traffic on the fortieth degree. The savages there, assisted by the Dutch, make war upon them, take them prisoners, and cruelly put them to death; and indeed they told us that the preceding year, while making war, they captured three of the Dutch, who were assisting their enemies, [137] as we do the Attigouautans, and while in action one of their own men was killed. Nevertheless they did not fail to send back the three Dutch prisoners, without doing them any harm, supposing that they belonged to our party, since they had no knowledge of us except by hearsay, never having seen a Christian; otherwise, they said, these three prisoners would not have got off so easily, and would not escape again should they surprise and take them. This nation is very warlike, as those of the nation of the Attigouautans maintain. They have only three villages, which are in the midst of more than twenty others, on which they make war without assistance from their friends; for they are obliged to pass through the thickly settled country of the Chouontouaroüon,[138] or else they would have to make a very long circuit.

After arriving at the village, it was necessary for me to remain until the men of war should come from the surrounding villages, so that we might be off as soon as possible. During this time there was a constant succession of banquets and dances on account of the joy they experienced at seeing me so determined to assist them in their war, just as if they were already assured of victory.

The greater portion of our men having assembled, we set out from the village on the first day of September, and passed along the shore of a small lake, [139] distant three leagues from the village, where they catch large quantities of fish, which they preserve for the winter. There is another lake, [140] closely adjoining, which is twenty-five leagues in circuit, and slows into the small one by a strait, where the above mentioned extensive fishing is carried on. This is done by means of a large number of stakes which almost close the strait, only some little openings being left where they place their nets, in which the fish are caught. These two lakes discharge into the *Mer Douce*. We remained some time in this place to await the rest of our savages. When they were all assembled, with their arms, meal, and necessaries, it was decided to choose some of the most resolute men to compose a party to go and give notice of our departure to those who were to assist us with five hundred men, that they might join us, and that we might appear together before the fort of the enemy. This decision having been made, they dispatched two canoes, with twelve of the most stalwart savages, and also with one of our interpreters, [141] who asked me to permit him to make the journey, which I readily accorded, inasmuch as he was led to do so of his own will, and as he might in this way see their country and get a knowledge of the people living there. The danger, however, was not small, since it was necessary to pass through the midst of enemies. They set out on the 8th of the month, and on the 10th following there was a heavy white frost.

We continued our journey towards the enemy, and went some five or six leagues through these lakes, [142] when the savages carried their canoes about ten leagues by land. We then came to another lake, [143] six to seven leagues in length and three broad. From this flows a river which discharges into the great lake of the Entouhonorons. After traversing this lake we passed a fall, and continuing our course down this river for about sixty-four leagues [144] entered the lake of the Entouhonorons, having passed, on our way by land, five falls, some being from four to five leagues long. We also passed several lakes of considerable size, through which the river passes. The latter is large and very abundant in good fish.

It is certain that all this region is very fine and pleasant. Along the banks it seems as if the trees had been set out for ornament in most places, and that all these tracts were in former times inhabited by savages, who were subsequently compelled to abandon them from fear of their enemies. Vines and nut-trees are here very numerous. Grapes mature, yet there is always a very pungent tartness which is felt remaining in the throat when one eats them in large quantities, arising from defect of cultivation. These localities are very pleasant when cleared up.

Stags and bears are here very abundant. We tried the hunt and captured a large number as we journeyed down. It was done in this way. They place four or five hundred savages in line in the woods, so that they extend to certain points on the river; then marching in order with bow and arrow in hand, shouting and making a great noise in order to frighten the beasts, they continue to advance until they come to the end of the point. Then all the animals between the point and the hunters are forced to throw themselves into the water, as many at least as do not fall by the arrows shot at them by the hunters. Meanwhile the savages, who are expressly arranged and posted in their canoes along the shore, easily approach the stags and other animals, tired out and greatly frightened in the chase, when they readily kill them with the spear heads attached to the extremity of a piece of wood of the shape of a half pike. This is the way they engage in the chase; and they do likewise on the islands where there are large quantities of game. I took especial pleasure in seeing them hunt thus and in observing their dexterity. Many animals were killed by the shot of the arquebus, at which the savages were greatly surprised. But it unfortunately happened that, while a stag was being killed, a savage, who chanced to come in range, was wounded by a shot of an arquebus. Thence a great commotion arose among them, which however subsided when some presents were given to the wounded. This is the usual manner of allaying and settling quarrels, and, in case of the death of the wounded, presents are given to the relatives of the one killed.

As to smaller game there is a large quantity of it in its season. There are also many cranes,[145] white as swans, and other varieties of birds like those in France.

We proceeded by short days' journeys as far as the shore of the lake of the Entouhonorons, constantly hunting as before mentioned. Here at its eastern extremity, which is the entrance to the great River St. Lawrence, we made the traverse, in latitude 43°, [146] where in the passage there are very large beautiful islands. We went about fourteen leagues in passing to the southern side of the lake towards the territory of the enemy. [147] The savages concealed all their canoes in the woods near the shore. We went some four leagues over a sandy strand, where I observed a very pleasant and beautiful country, intersected by many little streams and two small rivers, which discharge into the before-mentioned lake, also many ponds and meadows, where there was an endless amount of game, many vines, fine woods, and a large number of chestnut trees, whose fruit was still in the burr. The chestnuts are small, but of a good flavor. The country is covered with forests, which over its greater portion have not been cleared up. All the canoes being thus hidden, we left the border of the lake, [148] which is some eighty leagues long and twenty-five wide. [149] The greater portion of its shores is inhabited by savages. We continued our course by land for about twenty-five or thirty leagues. In the space of four days we crossed many brooks, and a river which proceeds from a lake that discharges into that of the Entouhonorons. [150] This lake is twenty-five or thirty leagues in circuit, contains some fine islands, and is the place where our enemies, the Iroquois, catch their fish, in which it abounds.

On the 9th of the month of October our savages going out to reconnoitre met eleven savages, whom they took prisoners. They consisted of four women, three boys, one girl, and three men, who were going fishing and were distant some four leagues from the fort of the enemy. Now it is to be noted that one of the chiefs, on seeing the prisoners, cut off the finger of one of these poor women as a beginning of their usual punishment; upon which I interposed and reprimanded the chief, Iroquet, representing to him that it was not the act of a warrior, as he declared himself to be, to conduct himself with cruelty towards women, who have no defence but their tears and that one should treat them with humanity on account of their helplessness and weakness; and I told him that on the contrary this act would be deemed to proceed from a base and brutal courage, and that if he committed any more of these cruelties he would not give me heart to assist them or favor them in the war. To which the only answer he gave me was that their enemies treated them in the same manner, but that, since this was displeasing to me, he would not do anything more to the women, although; he would to the men.

The next day, at three o'clock in the afternoon, we arrived before the fort [151] of their enemies, where the savages made some skirmishes with each other, although our design was not to disclose ourselves until the next day, which however the impatience of our savages would not permit, both on account of their desire to see fire opened upon their enemies, and also that they might rescue some of their own men who had become too closely engaged, and were hotly pressed. Then I approached the enemy, and although I had only a few men, yet we showed them what they had never seen nor heard before; for, as soon as they saw us and heard the arquebus shots and the balls whizzing in their ears, they withdrew speedily to their fort, carrying the dead and wounded in this charge. We also withdrew to our main body, with five or six wounded, one of whom died.

This done, we withdrew to the distance of cannon range, out of sight of the enemy, but contrary to my advice and to what they had promised me. This moved me to address them very rough and angry words in order to incite them to do their duty, foreseeing that if everything should go according to their whim and the guidance of their council, their utter ruin would be the result. Nevertheless I did not fail to send to them and propose means which they should use in order to get possession of their enemies.

These were, to make with certain kinds of wood a *cavalier*, which should be higher than the palisades. Upon this were to be placed four or five of our arquebusiers, who should keep up a constant fire over their palisades and galleries, which were well provided with stones, and by this means dislodge the enemy who might attack us from their galleries. Meanwhile orders were to be given to procure boards for making a sort of mantelet to protect our men from the arrows and stones of which the savages generally make use. These instruments, namely the cavalier and mantelets, were capable of being carried by a large number of men. One mantelet was so constructed that the water could not extinguish the fire, which might be set to the fort, under cover of the arquebusiers who were doing their duty on the cavalier. In this manner, I told them, we might be able to defend ourselves so that the enemy could not approach to extinguish the fire which we should set to their ramparts.

This proposition they thought good and very seasonable, and immediately proceeded to carry it out as I directed. In fact the next day they set to work, some to cut wood, others to gather it, for building and equipping the cavalier and mantelets. The work was promptly executed and in less than four hours, although the amount of wood they had collected for burning against the ramparts, in order to set fire to them, was very small. Their expectation was that the five hundred men who had promised to come would do so on this day, but doubt was felt about them, since they had not appeared at the rendezvous, as they had been charged to do, and as they had promised. This greatly troubled our savages; but seeing that they were sufficiently numerous to take the fort without other assistance, and thinking for my part that delay, if not in all things at least in many, is prejudicial, I urged them to attack it, representing to them that the enemy, having become aware of their force and our arms, which pierced whatever was proof against arrows, had begun to barricade themselves and cover themselves with strong pieces of wood, with which they were well provided and their village filled. I told them that the least delay was the best, since the enemy had already strengthened themselves very much; for their village was enclosed by four good palisades, which were made of great pieces of wood, interlaced with each other, with an opening of not more than half a foot between two, and which were thirty feet high, with galleries after the manner of a parapet, which they had furnished with double pieces of wood that were proof against our arquebus shots. Moreover it was near a pond where the water was abundant, and was well supplied with gutters, placed between each pair of palisades, to throw out water, which they had also under cover inside, in order to extinguish fire. Now this is the character of their fortifications and defences, which are much stronger than the villages of the Attigouautan and others.

We approached to attack the village, our cavalier being carried by two hundred of the strongest men, who put it down before the village at a pike's length off. I ordered three arquebusiers to mount upon it, who were well protected from the arrows and stones that could be shot or hurled at them. Meanwhile the enemy did not fail to send a large number of arrows which did not miss, and a great many stones, which they hurled from their palisades. Nevertheless a hot fire of arquebuses forced them to dislodge and abandon their galleries, in consequence of the cavalier which uncovered them, they not venturing to show themselves, but fighting under shelter. Now when the cavalier was carried forward, instead of bringing up the mantelets according to order, including that one under cover of which we were to set the fire, they abandoned them and began to scream at their enemies, shooting arrows into the fort, which in my opinion did little harm to the enemy.

But we must excuse them, for they are not warriors, and besides will have no discipline nor correction, and will do only what they please. Accordingly one of them set fire inconsiderately to the wood placed against the fort of the enemy, quite the wrong way and in the face of the wind, so that it produced no effect.

This fire being out, the greater part of the savages began to carry wood against the palisades, but in so small quantity that the fire could have no great effect. There also arose such disorder among them that one could not understand another, which greatly troubled me. In vain did I shout in their ears and remonstrate to my utmost with them as to the danger to which they exposed themselves by their bad behavior, but on account of the great noise they made they heard nothing. Seeing that shouting would only burst my head, and that my remonstrances were useless for putting a stop to the disorder, I did nothing more, but determined together with my men to do what we could, and fire upon such as we could see.

Meanwhile the enemy profited by our disorder to get water and pour it so abundantly that you would have said brooks were flowing through their spouts, the result of which was that the fire was instantly extinguished, while they did not cease shooting their arrows, which fell upon us like hail. But the men on the cavalier killed and maimed many. We were engaged in this combat about three hours, in which two of our chiefs and leading warriors were wounded, namely, one called *Ochateguain* and another *Orani*, together with some fifteen common warriors. The others, seeing their men and some of the chiefs wounded, now began to talk of a retreat without farther fighting, in expectation of the five hundred men, [152] whose arrival could not be much delayed. Thus they retreated, a disorderly rabble.

Moreover the chiefs have in fact no absolute control over their men, who are governed by their own will and follow their own fancy, which is the cause of their disorder and the ruin of all their undertakings; for, having determined upon anything with their leaders, it needs only the whim of a villain, or nothing at all, to lead them to break it off and form a new plan. Thus there is no concert of action among them, as can be seen by this expedition.

Now we withdrew into our fort, I having received two arrow wounds, one in the leg, the other in the knee, which caused me great inconvenience, aside from the severe pain. When they were all assembled, I addressed them some words of remonstrance on the disorder that had occurred. But all I said availed nothing, and had no effect upon them. They replied that many of their men had been wounded like myself, so that it would cause the others much trouble and inconvenience to carry them as they retreated, and that it was not possible to return again against their enemies, as I told them it was their duty to do. They agreed, however, to wait four days longer for the five hundred men who were to come; and, if they came, to make a second effort against their enemies, and execute better what I might tell them than they had done in the past. With this I had to content myself, to my great regret.

Herewith is indicated the manner in which they fortify their towns, from which representation it may be inferred that those of their friends and enemies are fortified in like manner.

The next day there was a violent wind, which lasted two days, and was very favorable for setting fire anew to the fort of the enemy which, although I urged them strongly, they were unwilling to do, as if they were afraid of getting the worst of it, and besides they pleaded their wounded as an excuse.

We remained in camp until the 16th of the month, [153] during which time there were some skirmishes between the enemy and our men, who were very often surrounded by the former, rather through their imprudence than from lack of courage; for I assure you that every time we went to the charge it was necessary for us to go and disengage them from the crowd, since they could only retreat under cover of our arquebusiers, whom the enemy greatly dreaded and feared; for as soon as they perceived any one of the arquebusiers they withdrew speedily, saying in a persuasive manner that we should not interfere in their combats, and that their enemies had very little courage to require us to assist them, with many other words of like tenor, in order to prevail upon us.

I have represented by figure E the manner in which they arm themselves in going to war.

After some days, seeing that the five hundred men did not come, they determined to depart, and enter upon their retreat as soon as possible. They proceeded to make a kind of basket for carrying the wounded, who are put into it crowded up in a heap, being bound and pinioned in such a manner that it is as impossible for them to move as for an infant in its swaddling clothes; but this is, not without causing the wounded much extreme pain. This I can say with truth from my own experience, having been carried some days, since I could not stand up, particularly on account of an arrow-wound which I had received in the knee. I never found myself in such a *gehenna* as during this time, for the pain which I suffered in consequence of the wound in my knee was nothing in comparison with that which I endured while I was carried bound and pinioned on the back of one of our savages; so that I lost my patience, and as soon as I could sustain myself, got out of this prison, or rather *gehenna*.

The enemy followed us about half a league, though at a distance, with the view of trying to take some of those composing the rear guard; but their efforts were vain, and they retired.

Now the only good point that I have seen in their mode of warfare is that they make their retreat very securely, placing all the wounded and aged in their centre, being well armed on the wings and in the rear, and continuing this order without interruption until they reach a place of security.

Their retreat was very long, being from twenty-five to thirty leagues, which caused the wounded much fatigue, as also those who carried them, although the latter relieved each other from time to time.

On the 18th day of the month there fell much snow and hail, accompanied by a strong wind, which greatly incommoded us. Nevertheless we succeeded in arriving at the shore of the lake of the Entouhonorons, at the place where our canoes were concealed, which we found all intact, for we had been afraid lest the enemy might have broken them up.

When they were all assembled, and I saw that they were ready to depart to their village, I begged them to take me to our settlement, which, though unwilling at first, they finally concluded to do, and sought four men to conduct me. Four men were found, who offered themselves of their own accord; for, as I have before said, the chiefs have no control over their men, in consequence of which they are often unable to do as they would like. Now the men having been found, it was necessary also to find a canoe, which was not to be had, each one needing his own, and there being no more than they required. This was far from being pleasant to me, but, on the contrary greatly annoyed me, since it led me to suspect some evil purpose, inasmuch as they had promised to conduct me to our settlement after their war. Moreover I was poorly prepared for spending the winter with them, or else should not have been concerned about the matter. But not being able to do anything, I was obliged to resign myself in patience. Now after some days I perceived that their plan was to keep me and my companions, not only as a security for themselves, for they feared their enemies, but also that I might listen to what took place in their councils and assemblies, and determine what they should do in the future against their enemies for their security and preservation.

The next day, the 28th of the month, they began to make preparations; some to go deer-hunting, others to hunt bears and beavers, others to go fishing, others to return to their villages. An abode and lodging were furnished me by one of the principal chiefs, called *D'Arontal*, with whom I already had some acquaintance. Having offered me his cabin, provisions, and accommodations, he set out also for the deer-hunt, which is esteemed by them the greatest and most noble one. After crossing, from the island, [154] the end of the lake, we entered a river [155] some twelve leagues in extent. They then carried their canoes by land some half a league, when we entered a lake [156] which was some ten or twelve leagues in circuit, where there was a large amount of game, as swans, [157] white cranes, [158] outardes, [159] ducks, teal, song-thrush, [160] larks, [161] snipe, [162] geese, [163] and several other kinds of fowl too numerous to mention. Of these I killed a great number, which stood us in good stead while waiting for the capture of a deer. From there we proceeded to a certain place some ten leagues distant, where our savages thought there were deer in abundance. Assembled there were some twenty-five savages, who set to building two or three cabins out of pieces of wood fitted to each other, the chinks of which they stopped up by means of moss to prevent the entrance of the air, covering them with the bark of trees.

When they had done this they went into the woods to a small forest of firs, where they made an enclosure in the form of a triangle, closed up on two sides and open on one. This enclosure was made of great stakes of wood closely pressed together, from eight to nine feet high, each of the sides being fifteen hundred paces long. At the extremity of this triangle there was a little enclosure, constantly diminishing in size, covered in part with boughs and with only an opening of five feet, about the width of a medium-sized door, into which the deer were to enter. They were so expeditious in their work, that in less than ten days they had their enclosure in readiness. Meanwhile other savages had gone fishing, catching trout and pike of prodigious size, and enough to meet all our wants.

All preparations being made, they set out half an hour before day to go into the wood, some half a league from the before-mentioned enclosure, separated from each other some eighty paces. Each had two sticks, which they struck together, and they marched in this order at a slow pace until they arrived at their enclosure. The deer hearing this noise flee before them until they reach the enclosure, into which the savages force them to go. Then they gradually unite on approaching the bay and opening of their triangle, the deer skirting the sides until they reach the end, to which the savages hotly pursue them, with bow and arrow in hand ready to let fly. On reaching the end of the triangle they begin to shout and imitate wolves, [164] which are numerous, and which devour the deer. The deer, hearing this frightful noise, are constrained to enter the retreat by the little opening, whither they are very hotly pursued by arrow shots. Having entered this retreat, which is so well closed and fastened that they can by no possibility get out, they are easily captured. I assure you that there is a singular pleasure in this chase, which took place every two days, and was so successful that, in the thirty-eight days [165] during which we were there, they captured one hundred and twenty deer, which they make good use of, reserving the fat for winter, which they use as we do butter, and taking away to their homes some of the flesh for their festivities.

They have other contrivances for capturing the deer; as snares, with which they kill many. You see depicted opposite the manner of their chase, enclosure, and snare. Out of the skins they make garments. Thus you see how we spent the time while waiting for the frost, that we might return the more easily, since the country is very marshy.

When they first went out hunting, I lost my way in the woods, having followed a certain bird that seemed to me peculiar. It had a beak like that of a parrot, and was of the size of a hen. It was entirely yellow, except the head which was red, and the wings which were blue, and it flew by intervals like a partridge. The desire to kill it led me to pursue it from tree to tree for a very long time, until it flew away in good earnest. Thus losing all hope, I desired to retrace my steps, but found none of our hunters, who had been constantly getting ahead, and had reached the enclosure. While trying to overtake them, and going, as it seemed to me, straight to where the enclosure was, I found myself lost in the woods, going now on this side now on that, without being able to recognize my position. The night coming on, I was obliged to spend it at the foot of a great tree, and in the morning set out and walked until three o'clock in the afternoon, when I came to a little pond of still water. Here I noticed some game, which I pursued, killing three or four birds, which were very acceptable, since I had had nothing to eat. Unfortunately for me there had been no sunshine for three days, nothing but rain and cloudy weather, which increased my trouble. Tired and exhausted I prepared to rest myself and cook the birds in order to alleviate the hunger which I began painfully to feel, and which by God's favor was appeased.

When I had made my repast I began to consider what I should do, and to pray God to give me the will and courage to sustain patiently my misfortune if I should be obliged to remain abandoned in this forest without counsel or consolation except the Divine goodness and mercy, and at the same time to exert myself to return to our hunters. Thus committing all to His mercy I gathered up renewed courage going here and there all day, without perceiving any foot-print or path, except those of wild beasts, of which I generally saw a good number. I was obliged to pass here this night also. Unfortunately I had forgotten to bring with me a small compass which would have put me on the right road, or nearly so. At the dawn of day, after a brief repast, I set out in order to find, if possible, some brook and follow it, thinking that it must of necessity flow into the river on the border of which our hunters were encamped. Having resolved upon this plan, I carried it out so well that at noon I found myself on the border of a little lake, about a league and a half in extent, where I killed some game, which was very timely for my wants; I had likewise remaining some eight or ten charges of powder, which was a great satisfaction.

I proceeded along the border of this lake to see where it discharged, and found a large brook, which I followed until five o'clock in the evening, when I heard a great noise, but on carefully listening failed to perceive clearly what it was. On hearing the noise, however, more distinctly, I concluded that it was a fall of water in the river which I was searching for. I proceeded nearer, and saw an opening, approaching which I found myself in a great and far-reaching meadow, where there was a large number of wild beasts, and looking to my right I perceived the river, broad and long. I looked to see if I could not recognize the place, and walking along on the meadow I noticed a little path where the savages carried their canoes. Finally, after careful observation, I recognized it as the same river, and that I had gone that way before.

I passed the night in better spirits than the previous ones, supping on the little I had. In the morning I re-examined the place where I was, and concluded from certain mountains on the border of the river that I had not been deceived, and that our hunters must be lower down by four or five good leagues. This distance I walked at my leisure along the border of the river, until I perceived the smoke of our hunters, where I arrived to the great pleasure not only of myself but of them, who were still searching for me, but had about given up all hopes of seeing me again. They begged me not to stray off from them any more, or never to forget to carry with me my compass, and they added: If you had not come, and we had not succeeded in finding you, we should never have gone again to the French, for fear of their accusing us of having killed you. After this he [166] was very careful of me when I went hunting, always giving me a savage as companion, who knew how to find again the place from which he started so well that it was something very remarkable.

To return to my subject: they have a kind of superstition in regard to this hunt; namely, they believe that if they should roast any of the meat taken in this way, or if any of the fat should fall into the fire, or if any of the bones should be thrown into it, they would not be able to capture any more deer. Accordingly they begged me to roast none of this meat, but I laughed at this and their way of doing. Yet, in order not to offend them, I cheerfully desisted, at least in their presence; though when they were out of sight I took some of the best and roasted it, attaching no credit to their superstitions. When I afterwards told them what I had done, they would not believe me, saying that they could not have taken any deer after the doing of such a thing.

On the fourth day of December we set out from this place, walking on the river, lakes, and ponds, which were frozen, and sometimes through the woods. Thus we went for nineteen days, undergoing much hardship and toil, both the savages, who were loaded with a hundred pounds, and myself, who carried a burden of twenty pounds, which in the long journey tired me very much. It is true that I was sometimes relieved by our savages, but nevertheless I suffered great discomfort. The savages, in order to go over the ice more easily, are accustomed to make a kind of wooden sledge, [167] on which they put their loads, which they easily and swiftly drag along. Some days after there was a thaw, which caused us much trouble and annoyance; for we had to go through pine forests full of brooks, ponds; marshes, and swamps, where many trees had been blown down upon each other. This caused us a thousand troubles and embarrassments, and great discomfort, as we were all the time wet to above our knees. We were four days in this plight, since in most places the ice would not bear. At last, on the 20th of the month, we succeeded in arriving at our village. [168] Here the Captain Yroquet had come to winter with his companions, who are Algonquins, also his son, whom he brought for the sake of treatment, since while hunting he had been seriously injured by a bear which he was trying to kill.

After resting some days I determined to go and visit Father Joseph, and to see in winter the people where he was, whom the war had not permitted me to see in the summer. I set out from this village on the 14th [169] of January following, thanking my host for the kindness he had shown me, and, taking formal leave of him, as I did not expect to see him again for three months.

The next day I Saw Father Joseph, [170] in his small house where he had taken up his abode, as I have before stated. I stayed with him some days, finding him deliberating about making a journey to the Petun people, as I had also thought of doing, although it was very disagreeable travelling in winter. We set out together on the fifteenth of February to go to that nation, where we arrived on the seventeenth of the month. [171] These Petun people plant the maize, called by us *blé de Turquie*, and have fixed abodes like the rest. We went to seven other villages of their neighbors and allies, with whom we contracted friendship, and who promised to come in good numbers to our settlement. They welcomed us with good cheer, making a banquet with meat and fish, as is their custom. To this the people from all quarters flocked in order to see us, showing many manifestations of friendship, and accompanying us on the greater part of our way back. The country is diversified with pleasant slopes and plains. They were beginning to build two villages, through which we passed, and which were situated in the midst of the woods, because of the convenience [172] of building and fortifying their towns there. These people live like the Attignouaatitans, [173] and have the same customs. They are situated near the Nation Neutre, [174] which are powerful and occupy a great extent of country. After visiting these people, we set out from that place, and went to a nation of savages, whom we named *Cheveux Relevés* [175] They were very happy to see us again, and we entered into friendship with them, while they in return promised to come and see us, namely at the habitation in this place.

It has seemed to me desirable to describe them and their country, their customs and mode of life. In the first place they are at war with another nation of savages, called Asistagueroüon, [176] which means *Gens de Feu*, who are distant from them ten days' journey. I informed myself accordingly very particularly in regard to their country and the tribes living there, as also to their character and numbers. The people of this nation are very numerous, and are for the most part great warriors, hunters, and fishermen. They have several chiefs, each ruling in his own district. In general they plant Indian corn, and other cereals. They are hunters who go in troops to various regions and countries, where they traffic with other nations, distant four or five hundred leagues. They are the cleanest savages in their household affairs that I have ever seen, and are very industrious in making a kind of mat, which constitutes their Turkish carpets. The women have the body covered, but the men go uncovered, with the exception of a fur robe in the form of a cloak, which they usually leave off in summer. The women and girls are not more moved at seeing them thus, than if they saw nothing unusual. The women live very happily with their husbands. They have the following custom when they have their catamenia: the wives withdraw from their husbands, or the daughter from her father and mother and other relatives, and go to certain small houses. There they remain in retirement, awaiting their time, without any company of men, who bring them food and necessaries until their return. Thus it is known who have their catamenia and who have not. This tribe is accustomed more than others to celebrate great banquets. They gave us good cheer and welcomed us very cordially, earnestly begging me to assist them against their enemies, who dwell on the banks of the *Mer Douce*, two hundred leagues distant; to which I replied that they must wait until another time, as I was not provided with the necessary means. They were at a loss how to welcome us. I have represented them in figure C as they go to war.

There is, also, at a distance of a two days' journey from them, in a southerly direction, another savage nation, that produces a large amount of tobacco. This is called *Nation Neutre*. They number four thousand warriors, and dwell westward of the lake of the Entouhonorons, which is from eighty to a hundred leagues in extent. They, however, assist the *Cheveux Relevés* against the *Gens de Feu*. But with the Iroquois and our allies they are at peace, and preserve a neutrality. There is a cordial understanding towards both of these nations, and they do not venture to engage in any dispute or quarrel, but on the contrary often eat and drink with them like good friends. I was very desirous of visiting this nation, but the people where we were dissuaded me from it, saying that the year before one of our men had killed one of them, when we were at war with the Entouhonorons, which offended them; and they informed us that they are much inclined to revenge, not concerning themselves as to who struck the blow, but inflicting the penalty upon the first one they meet of the nation, even though one of their friends, when they succeed in catching him, unless harmony has been previously restored between them, and gifts and presents bestowed upon the relatives of the deceased. Thus I was prevented for the time being from going, although some of this nation assured us that they would do us no harm for the reason assigned above.

Thus we were led to return the same way we had come, and continuing my journey, I reached the nation of the *Pisierinii,* [177] who had promised to conduct me farther on in the prosecution of my plans and explorations. But I was prevented by the intelligence which came from our great village and the Algonquins, where Captain Yroquet was, namely, that the people of the nation of the Atignouaatitans [178] had placed in his hands a prisoner of a hostile nation, in the expectation that this Captain Yroquet would exercise on the prisoner the revenge usual among them. But they said that, instead of doing so, he had not only set him at liberty, but, having found him apt, and an excellent hunter, had treated him as his son, on account of which the Atignouaatitans had become jealous and resolved upon vengeance, and had in fact appointed a man to go and kill this prisoner, allied as he was. As he was put to death in the presence of the chiefs of the Algonquin nation, they, indignant at such an act and moved to anger, killed on the spot this rash murderer; whereupon the Atignouaatitans feeling themselves insulted, seeing one of their comrades dead, seized their arms and went to the tents of the Algonquins, who were passing the winter near the above mentioned village, and belabored them severely, Captain Yroquet receiving two arrow wounds. At another time they pillaged some of the cabins of the Algonquins before the latter could place themselves in a state of defence, so that they had not an equal chance. Notwithstanding this they were not reconciled to the Algonquins, who for securing peace had given the Atignouaatitans fifty necklaces of porcelain and a hundred branches of the same [179] which they value highly, and likewise a number of kettles and axes, together with two female prisoners in place of the dead man.

They were, in a word, still in a state of violent animosity. The Algonquins were obliged to suffer patiently this great rage, and feared that they might all be killed, not feeling any security, notwithstanding their gifts, until they should be differently situated. This intelligence greatly disturbed me, when I considered the harm that might arise not only to them, but to us as well, who were in their country.

I then met two or three savages of our large village, who earnestly entreated me to go to them in order to effect a reconciliation, declaring that if I did not go none of them would come to us any more, since they were at war with the Algonquins and regarded us as their friends. In view of this I set out as soon as possible, and visited on my way the Nipissings to ascertain when they would be ready for the journey to the north, which I found broken off on account of these quarrels and hostilities, as my interpreter gave me to understand, who said that Captain Yroquet had come among all these tribes to find and await me. He had requested them to be at the habitation of the French at the same time with himself to see what agreement could be made between them and the Atignouaatitans, and to postpone the journey to the north to another time. Moreover, Yroquet had given porcelain to break off this journey. They promised us to be at our habitation at the same time as the others.

If ever there was one greatly disheartened it was myself, since I had been waiting to see this year what during many preceding ones I had been seeking for with great toil and effort, through so many fatigues and risks of my life. But realizing that I could not help the matter, and that everything depended on the will of God, I comforted myself, resolving to see it in a short time. I had such sure information that I could not doubt the report of these people, who go to traffic with others dwelling in those northern regions, a great part of whom live in a place very abundant in the chase, and where there are great numbers of large animals, the skins of several of which I saw, and which I concluded were buffaloes [180] from their representation of their form. Fishing is also very abundant there. This journey requires forty days, as well in returning as in going.

I set out towards our above-mentioned village on the 15th of February, taking with me six of our men. Having arrived at that place the inhabitants were greatly pleased, as also the Algonquins, whom

I sent our interpreter to visit in order to ascertain how everything had taken place on both sides, for I did not wish to go myself that I might give no ground for suspicion to either party.

Two days were spent in hearing from both sides how everything had taken place. After this the principal men and seniors of the place came away with us, and we all together went to the Algonquins. Here in one of their cabins, where several of the leading men were assembled, they all, after some talk, agreed to come and accept all that might be said by me as arbiter in the matter, and to carry out what I might propose.

Then I gathered the views of each one, obtaining and investigating the wishes and inclinations of both parties, and ascertained that all they wanted was peace.

I set forth to them that the best course was to become reconciled and remain friends, since being united and bound together they could the more easily withstand their enemies; and as I went away I begged them not to ask me to effect their reconciliation if they did not intend to follow in all respects the advice I should give them in regard to this dispute, since they had done me the honor to request my opinion. Whereupon they told me anew that they had not desired my return for any other reason. I for my part thought that if I should not reconcile and pacify them they would separate ill disposed towards each other, each party thinking itself in the right. I reflected, also, that they would not have gone to their cabins if I had not been with them, nor to the French if I had not interested myself and taken, so to speak, the charge and conduct of their affairs. Upon this I said to them that as for myself I proposed to go with my host, who had always treated me well, and that I could with difficulty find one so good; for it was on him that the Algonquins laid the blame, saying that he was the only captain who had caused the taking up of arms. Much was said by both sides, and finally it was concluded that I should tell them what seemed to me best, and give them my advice.

Since I saw now from what was said that they referred the whole matter to my own decision as to that of a father, and promised that in the future I might dispose of them as I thought best, referring the whole matter to my judgment for settlement, I replied that I was very glad to see them so inclined to follow my advice, and assured them that it should be only for the best interests of the tribes.

Moreover I told them, I had been greatly disturbed at hearing the further sad intelligence, namely the death of one of their relatives and friends, whom we regarded as one of our own, which might have caused a great calamity resulting in nothing but perpetual wars between both parties, with various and serious disasters and a rupture of their friendship, in consequence of which the French would be deprived of seeing them and of intercourse with them, and be obliged to enter into alliance with other nations; since we loved each other as brothers, leaving to God the punishment of those meriting it.

I proceeded to say to them, that this mode of action between two nations, who were, as they acknowledged, friendly to each other, was unworthy of reasoning men, but rather characteristic of brute beasts. I represented to them, moreover, that they were enough occupied in repelling their enemies who pursued them, in routing them as often as possible, in pursuing them to their villages and taking them prisoners; and that these enemies, seeing divisions and wars among them, would be delighted and derive great advantage therefrom; and be led to lay new and pernicious plans, in the hope of soon being able to see their ruin, or at least their enfeebling through one another, which would be the truest and easiest way for them to conquer and become masters of their territories, since they did not assist each other.

I told them likewise that they did not realize the harm that might befall them from thus acting; that on account of the death of one man they hazarded the lives of ten thousand, and ran the risk of being reduced to perpetual slavery; that, although in fact one man was of great value, yet they ought to consider how he had been killed, and that it was not with deliberate purpose, nor for the sake of inciting a civil war, it being only too evident that the dead man had first offended, since with deliberate purpose he had killed the prisoner in their cabins, a most audacious thing, even if the latter were an enemy. This aroused the Algonquins, who, seeing a man that had been so bold as to kill in their own cabins another to whom they had given liberty and treated as one of themselves, were carried away with passion; and some, more excited than the rest, advanced, and, unable to restrain or control their wrath, killed the man in question. Nevertheless they had no ill feeling at all towards the nation as a whole, and did not extend their purposes beyond the audacious one, who, they thought, fully deserved what he had wantonly earned.

And besides I told them they must confider that the Entouhonoron, finding himself wounded by two blows in the stomach, tore from his wound the knife which his enemy had left there and gave the latter two blows, as I had been informed; so that in fact one could not tell whether it was really the Algonquins who had committed the murder. And in order to show to the Attigouantans that the Algonquins did not love the prisoner, and that Yroquet did not bear towards him the affection which they were disposed to think, I reminded them that they had eaten him, as he had inflicted blows with a knife upon his enemy; a thing, however, unworthy of a human being, but rather characteristic of brute beasts.

I told them also that the Algonquins very much regretted all that had taken place, and that, if they had supposed such a thing would have happened, they would have sacrificed this Iroquois for their satisfaction. I reminded them likewise that they had made recompense for this death and offence, if so it should be called, by large presents and two prisoners, on which account they had no reason at present to complain, and ought to restrain themselves and act more mildly towards the Algonquins, their friends. I told them that, since they had promised to submit every thing to arbitration, I entreated them to forget all that had passed between them and never to think of it again, nor bear any hatred or ill will on account of it to each other, but to live good friends as before, by doing which they would constrain us to love them and assist them as I had done in the past. But in case they should not be pleased with my advice, I requested them to come, in as large numbers as possible, to our settlement, so that there, in the presence of all the captains of vessels, our friendship might be ratified anew, and measures taken to secure them from their enemies, a thing which they ought to consider.

Then they began to say that I had spoken well, and that they would adhere to what I had said, and all went away to their cabins, apparently satisfied, excepting the Algonquins, who broke up and proceeded to their village, but who, as it seemed to me, appeared to be not entirely satisfied, since they said among themselves that they would not come to winter again in these places, the death of these two men having cost them too dearly. As for myself, I returned to my host, in whom I endeavored to inspire all the courage I could, in order to induce him to come to our settlement, and bring with him all those of his country.

During the winter, which lasted four months, I had sufficient leisure to observe their country, customs, dress, manner of living, the character of their assemblies, and other things which I should like to describe. But it is necessary first to speak of the situation of the country in general and its divisions, also of the location of the tribes and the distances between them.

The country extends in length, in the direction from east to west, nearly four hundred and fifty leagues, and some eighty or a hundred leagues in breadth from north to south, from latitude 41° to 48° or 49° [181] This region is almost an island, surrounded by the great river Saint Lawrence, which passes through several lakes of great extent, on the shores of which dwell various tribes speaking different languages, having fixed abodes, and all fond of the cultivation of the soil, but with various modes of life, and customs, some better than others. On the shore north of this great river, extending westerly some hundred leagues towards the Attigouantans, [182] there are very high mountains, and the air is more temperate than in any other part of these regions, the latitude being 41°. All these places abound in game, such as stags, caribous, elks, does, [183] buffaloes, bears, wolves, beavers, foxes, minxes, [184] weasels, [185] and many other kinds of animals which we do not have in France. Fishing is abundant, there being many varieties, both those which we have in France, as also others which we have not. There are likewise many birds in their time and season. The country is traversed by numerous rivers, brooks, and ponds, connecting with each other and finally emptying into the river St. Lawrence and the lakes through which it passes. The country is very pleasant in spring, is covered with extensive and lofty forests, and filled with wood similar to that which we have in France, although in many places there is much cleared land, where they plant Indian corn. This region also abounds in meadows, lowlands, and marshes, which furnish food for the animals before mentioned.

The country north of the great river is very rough and mountainous, and extends in latitude from 47° to 49°, and in places abounds in rocks. [186] So far as I could make out, these regions are inhabited by savages, who wander through the country, not engaging in the cultivation of the soil, nor doing anything, or at least as good as nothing. But they are hunters, now in one place, now in another, the region being very cold and disagreeable. This land on the north is in latitude 49° and extends over six hundred leagues in breadth from east to west, of parts of which we have full knowledge. There are also many fine large rivers rising in this region and discharging into the before-mentioned river, together with an infinite number of fine meadows, lakes, and ponds, through which they pass, where there is an abundance of fish. There are likewise numerous islands which are for the most part cleared up and very pleasant, the most of them containing great quantities of vines and wild fruits.

With regard to the regions further west, we cannot well determine their extent, since the people here have no knowledge of them except for two or three hundred leagues or more westerly, from whence comes the great river, which passes, among other places, through a lake having an extent of nearly thirty days' journey by canoe, namely that which we have called the *Mer Douce*. This is of great extent, being nearly four hundred leagues long. Inasmuch as the savages, with whom we are on friendly terms, are at war with other nations on the west of this great lake, we cannot obtain a more complete knowledge of them, except as they have told us several times that some prisoners from the distance of a hundred leagues had reported that there were tribes there like ourselves in color and in other respects. Through them they have seen the hair of these people which is very light, and which they esteem highly, saying that it is like our own. I can only conjecture in regard to this, that the people they say resemble us were those more civilized than themselves. It would require actual presence to ascertain the truth in regard to this matter. But assistance is needed, and it is only men of means, leisure, and energy, who could or would undertake to promote this enterprise so that a full exploration of these places might be made, affording us a complete knowledge of them.

In regard to the region south of the great river it is very thickly settled, much more so than that on the north, and by tribes who are at war with each other. The country is very pleasant, much more so than that on the northern border, and the air is more temperate. There are many kinds of trees and fruits not found north of the river, while there are many things on the north side, in compensation, not found on the south. The regions towards the east are sufficiently well known, inasmuch as the ocean borders these places. These are the coasts of Labrador, Newfoundland, Cape Breton, La Cadie, and the Almouchiquois, [187] places well known, as I have treated of them sufficiently in the narrative of my previous Voyages, as likewise of the people living there, on which account I shall not speak of them in this treatise, my object being only to make a succinct and true report of what I have seen in addition.

The country of the nation of the Attigouantans is in latitude 44° 30', and extends two hundred and thirty leagues [188] in length westerly, and ten in breadth. It contains eighteen villages, six of which are enclosed and fortified by palisades of wood in triple rows, bound together, on the top of which are galleries, which they provide with stones and water; the former to hurl upon their enemies and the latter to extinguish the fire which their enemies may set to the palisades. The country is pleasant, most of it cleared up. It has the shape of Brittany, and is similarly situated, being almost surrounded by the *Mer Douce* [189] They assume that these eighteen villages are inhabited by two thousand warriors, not including the common mass which amounts to perhaps thirty thousand souls.

Their cabins are in the shape of tunnels or arbors, and are covered with the bark of trees. They are from twenty-five to thirty fathoms long, more or less, and six wide, having a passage-way through the middle from ten to twelve feet wide, which extends from one end to the other. On the two sides there is a kind of bench, four feet high, where they sleep in summer, in order to avoid the annoyance of the fleas, of which there are great numbers. In winter they sleep on the ground on mats near the fire, so as to be warmer than they would be on the platform. They lay up a stock of dry wood, with which they fill their cabins, to burn in winter. At the extremity of the cabins there is a space, where they preserve their Indian corn, which they put into great casks made of the bark of trees and placed in the middle of their encampment. They have pieces of wood suspended, on which they put their clothes, provisions, and other things, for fear of the mice, of which there are great numbers. In one of these cabins there may be twelve fires, and twenty-four families. It smokes excessively, from which it follows that many receive serious injury to the eyes, so that they lose their sight towards the close of life. There is no window nor any opening, except that in the upper part of their cabins for the smoke to escape.

This is all that I have been able to learn about their mode of life; and I have described to you fully the kind of dwelling of these people, as far as I have been able to learn it, which is the same as that of all the tribes living in these regions. They sometimes change their villages at intervals of ten, twenty, or thirty years, and transfer them to a distance of one, two, or three leagues from the preceding situation, [190] except when compelled by their enemies to dislodge, in which case they retire to a greater distance, as the Antouhonorons, who went some forty to fifty leagues. This is the form of their dwellings, which are separated from each other some three or four paces, for fear of fire, of which they are in great dread.

Their life is a miserable one in comparison with our own; but they are happy among themselves, not having experienced anything better, and not imagining that anything more excellent is to be found. Their principal articles of food are Indian corn and Brazilian beans, [191] which they prepare in various ways. By braying in a wooden mortar they reduce the corn to meal. They remove the bran by means of fans made of the bark of trees. From this meal they make bread, using also beans which they first boil, as they do the Indian corn for soup, so that they may be more easily crushed. Then they mix all together, sometimes adding blueberries [192] or dry raspberries, and sometimes pieces of deer's fat, though not often, as this is scarce with them. After steeping the whole in lukewarm water, they make bread in the form of bannocks or pies, which they bake in the ashes. After they are baked they wash them, and from these they often make others by wrapping them in corn leaves, which they fasten to them, and then putting them in boiling water.

But this is not their most common kind. They make another, which they call *migan*, which is as follows: They take the pounded

Indian corn, without removing the bran, and put two or three handfuls of it in an earthen pot full of water. This they boil, stirring it from time to time, that it may not burn nor adhere to the pot. Then they put into the pot a small quantity of fish, fresh or dry, according to the season, to give a flavor to the *migan*, as they call it. They make it very often, although it smells badly, especially in winter, either because they do not know how to prepare it rightly, or do not wish to take the trouble to do so. They make two kinds of it, and prepare it very well when they choose. When they use fish the *migan* does not smell badly, but only when it is made with venison. After it is all cooked, they take out the fish, pound it very fine, and then put it all together into the pot, not taking the trouble to remove the appendages, scales, or inwards, as we do, which generally causes a bad taste. It being thus prepared, they deal out to each one his portion. This *migan* is very thin, and without much substance, as may be well supposed. As for drink, there is no need of it, the *migan* being sufficiently thin of itself.

They have another kind of *migan*, namely, they roast new corn before it is ripe, which they preserve and cook whole with fish, or flesh when they have it. Another way is this: they take Indian corn, which is very dry, roast it in the ashes, then bray it and reduce it to meal as in the former case. This they lay up for the journeys which they undertake here and there. The *migan* made in the latter manner is the best according to my taste. Figure H shows the women braying their Indian corn. In preparing it, they cook a large quantity of fish and meat, which they cut into pieces and put into great kettles, which they fill with water and let it all boil well. When this is done, they gather with a spoon from the surface the fat which comes from the meat and fish. Then they put in the meal of the roasted corn, constantly stirring it until the *migan* is cooked and thick as soup. They give to each one a portion, together with a spoonful of the fat. This dish they are accustomed to prepare for banquets, but they do not generally make it.

Now the corn freshly roasted, as above described, is highly esteemed among them. They eat also beans, which they boil with the mass of the roasted flour, mixing in a little fat and fish. Dogs are in request at their banquets, which they often celebrate among themselves, especially in winter, when they are at leisure. In case they go hunting for deer or go fishing, they lay aside what they get for celebrating these banquets, nothing remaining in their cabins but the usual thin *migan*, resembling bran and water, such as is given to hogs to eat.

They have another way of eating the Indian corn. In preparing it, they take it in the ear and put it in water under the mud, leaving it two or three months in this state until they think it is putrefied. Then they remove it, and eat it boiled with meat or fish. They also roast it, and it is better so than boiled. But I assure you that there is nothing that smells so badly as this corn as it comes from the water all muddy. Yet the women and children take it and suck it like sugar-cane, nothing seeming to them to taste better, as they show by their manner. In general they have two meals a day. As for ourselves, we fasted all of Lent and longer, in order to influence them by our example. But it was time lost.

They also fatten bears, which they keep two or three years, for the purpose of their banquets. I observed that if this people had domestic animals they would be interested in them and care for them very well, and I showed them the way to keep them, which would be an easy thing for them, since they have good grazing grounds in their country, and in large quantities, for all kinds of animals, horses, oxen, cows, sheep, swine, and other kinds, for lack of which one would consider them badly off, as they seem to be. Yet with all their drawbacks, they seem to me to live happily among themselves, since their only ambition is to live and support themselves, and they lead a more settled life than those who wander through the forests like brute beasts. They eat many squashes, [193] which they boil, and roast in the ashes.

In regard to their dress, they have various kinds and styles made of the skins of wild beasts, both those which they capture themselves, and others which they get in exchange for their Indian corn, meal, porcelain, and fishing-nets from the Algonquins, Nipissings, and other tribes, which are hunters having no fixed abodes. All their clothes are of one uniform shape, not varied by any new styles. They prepare and fit very well the skins, making their breeches of deer-skin rather large, and their stockings of another piece, which extend up to the middle and have many folds. Their shoes are made of the skins of deer, bears, and beaver, of which they use great numbers. Besides, they have a robe of the same fur, in the form of a cloak, which they wear in the Irish or Egyptian style, with sleeves which are attached with a string behind. This is the way they are dressed in winter, as is seen in figure D. When they go into the fields, they gird up their robe about the body; but when in the village, they leave off their sleeves and do not gird themselves. The Milan trimmings for decorating their garments are made of glue and the scrapings of the before-mentioned skins, of which they make bands in various styles according to their fancy, putting in places bands of red and brown color amid those of the glue, which always keep a whitish appearance, not losing at all their shape, however dirty they may get. There are those among these nations who are much more skilful than others in fitting the skins, and ingenious in inventing ornaments to put on their garments. It is our Montagnais and Algonquins, above all others, who take more pains in this matter. They put on their robes bands of porcupine quills, which they dye a very fine scarlet color. [194] They value these bands very highly, and detach them so that they may serve for other robes when they wish to make a change. They also make use of them to adorn the face, in order to give it a more graceful appearance whenever they wish particularly to decorate themselves.

Most of them paint the face black and red. These colors they mix with oil made from the seed of the sun-flower, or with bear's fat or that of other animals. They also dye their hair, which some wear long, others short, others on one side only. The women and girls always wear their hair in one uniform style. They are dressed like men, except that they always have their robes girt about them, which extend down to the knee. They are not at all ashamed to expose the body from the middle up and from the knees down, unlike the men, the rest being always covered. They are loaded with quantities of porcelain, in the shape of necklaces and chains, which they arrange in the front of their robes and attach to their waists. They also wear bracelets and ear-rings. They have their hair carefully combed, dyed, and oiled. Thus they go to the dance, with a knot of their hair behind bound up with eel-skin, which they use as a cord. Sometimes they put on plates a foot square, covered with porcelain, which hang on the back. Thus gaily dressed and habited, they delight to appear in the dance, to which their fathers and mothers send them, forgetting nothing that they can devise to embellish and set off their daughters. I can testify that I have seen at dances a girl who had more than twelve pounds of porcelain on her person, not including the other bagatelles with which they are loaded and bedecked. In the illustration already cited, F shows the dress of the women, G that of the girls attired for the dance.

All these people have a very jovial disposition, although there are many of them who have a sad and gloomy look. Their bodies are well proportioned. Some of the men and women are well formed, strong, and robust. There is a moderate number of pleasing and pretty girls, in respect to figure, color, and expression, all being in harmony. Their blood is but little deteriorated, except when they are old. There are among these tribes powerful women of extraordinary height These have almost the entire care of the house and work; namely, they till the land, plant the Indian corn, lay up a store of wood for the winter, beat the hemp and spin it, making from the thread fishing-nets and other useful things. The women harvest the corn, house it, prepare it for eating, and attend to household matters. Moreover they are expected to attend their husbands from place to place in the fields, filling the office of pack-mule in carrying the baggage, and to do a thousand other things. All the men do is to hunt for deer and other animals, fish, make their cabins, and go to war. Having done these things, they then go to other tribes with which they are acquainted to traffic and make exchanges. On their return, they give themselves up to festivities and dances, which they give to each other, and when these are over they go to sleep, which they like to do best of all things.

They have some sort of marriage, which is as follows: when a girl has reached the age of eleven, twelve, thirteen, fourteen, or fifteen years she has suitors, more or less according to her attractions, who woo her for some time. After this, the consent of their fathers and mothers is asked, to whose will the girls often do not submit, although the most discreet and considerate do so. The lover or suitor presents to the girl some necklaces, chains, and bracelets of porcelain. If the girl finds the suitor agreeable, she receives the present. Then the lover comes and remains with her three or four nights, without saying anything to her during the time. They receive thus the fruit of their affections. Whence it happens very often that, after from eight to fifteen days, if they cannot agree, she quits her suitor, who forfeits his necklaces and other presents that he has made, having received in return only a meagre satisfaction. Being thus disappointed in his hopes, the man seeks another woman, and the girl another suitor, if it seems to them desirable. Thus they continue to do until a favorable union is formed. It sometimes happens that a girl thus passes her entire youth, having more than twenty mates, which twenty are not alone in the enjoyment of the creature, mated though they are; for when night comes the young women run from one cabin to another, as do also the young men on their part, going where it seems good to them, but always without any violence, referring the whole matter to the pleasure of the woman. Their mates will do likewise to their women-neighbors, no jealousy arising among them on that account, nor do they incur any reproach or insult, such being the custom of the country.

Now the time when they do not leave their mates is when they have children. The preceding mate returns to her, renews the affection and friendship which he had borne her in the past, asserting that it is greater than that of any other one, and that the child she has is his and of his begetting. The next says the same to her. In time, the victory is with the stronger, who takes the woman for his wife. Thus it depends upon the choice of the woman to take and accept him who shall please her best, having meantime in her searching and loves gained much porcelain and, besides, the choice of a husband. The woman remains with him without leaving him; or if she do leave him, for he is on trial, it must be for some good reason other than impotence. But while with this husband, she does not cease to give herself free rein, yet remains always at home, keeping up a good appearance. Thus the children which they have together, born from such a woman, cannot be sure of their legitimacy. Accordingly, in view of this uncertainty, it is their custom that the children never succeed to the property and honors of their fathers, there being doubt, as above indicated, as to their paternity. They make, however, the children of their sisters, from whom they are known to have issued, their successors and heirs.

The following is the way they nourish and bring up their children: they place them during the day on a little wooden board, wrapping them up in furs or skins. To this board they bind them, placing them in an erect position, and leaving a little opening for the child to do its necessities. If it is a girl, they put a leaf of Indian corn between the thighs, which presses against its privates. The extremity of the leaf is carried outside in a turned position, so that the water of the child runs off on it without inconvenience. They put also under the children the down of certain reeds that we call hare's-foot, on which they rest very softly. They also clean them with the same down. As an ornament for the child, they adorn the board with beads, which they also put on its neck, however small it may be. At night they put it to bed, entirely naked, between the father and mother. It may be regarded as a great miracle that God should thus preserve it so that no harm befalls it, as might be expected, from suffocation, while the father and mother are in deep sleep, but that rarely happens. The children have great freedom among these tribes. The fathers and mothers indulge them too much, and never punish them. Accordingly they are so bad and of so vicious a nature, that they often strike their mothers and others. The most vicious, when they have acquired the strength and power, strike their fathers. They do this whenever the father or mother does anything that does not please them. This is a sort of curse that God inflicts upon them.

In respect to laws, I have not been able to find out that they have any, or anything that approaches them, inasmuch as there is not among them any correction, punishment, or censure of evil-doers except in the way of vengeance, when they return evil for evil, not by rule but by passion, which produces among them conflicts and differences, which occur very frequently.

Moreover, they do not recognize any divinity, or worship any God and believe in anything whatever, but live like brute beasts. They have, however, some respect for the devil, or something so called, which is a matter of uncertainty, since the word which they use thus has various significations and comprises in itself various things. It is accordingly difficult to determine whether they mean the devil or something else, but what especially leads to the belief that what they mean is the devil is this: whenever they see a man doing something extraordinary, or who is more capable than usual, or is a valiant warrior, or furthermore who is in a rage as if out of his reason and senses, they call him *oqui*, or, as we should say, a great knowing spirit, or a great devil. However this may be, they have certain persons, who are the *oqui*, or, as the Algonquins and Montagnais call them, *manitous*; and persons of this kind are the medicine-men, who heal the sick, bind up the wounded, and predict future events, who in fine practise all abuses and illusions of the devil to deceive and delude them. These *oquis* or conjurers persuade their patients and the sick to make, or have made banquets and ceremonies that they may be the sooner healed, their object being to participate in them finally themselves and get the principal benefit therefrom. Under the pretence of a more speedy cure, they likewise cause them to observe various other ceremonies, which I shall hereafter speak of in the proper place. These are the people in whom they put especial confidence, but it is rare that they are possessed of the devil and tormented like other savages living more remote than themselves.

This gives additional reason and ground to believe that their conversion to the knowledge of God would be more easy, if their country were inhabited by persons who would take the trouble and pains to instruct them. But it is not enough to send to them friars, unless there are those to support and assist them. For although these people have the desire to-day to know what God is, to-morrow this disposition will change when they are obliged to lay aside and bring under their foul ways, their dissolute manners, and their savage indulgences. So that there is need of people and families to keep them in the way of duty, to constrain them through mildness to do better, and to move them by good example to mend their lives. Father Joseph [195] and myself have many times conferred with them in regard to our belief, laws, and customs. They listened attentively in their assemblies, sometimes saying to us: You say things that pass our knowledge, and which we cannot understand by words, being beyond our comprehension; but if you would do us a service come and dwell in this country, bringing your wives and children, and when they are here we shall see how you serve the God you worship, and how you live with your wives and children, how you cultivate and plant the soil, how you obey your laws, how you take care of animals, and how you manufacture all that we see proceeding from your inventive skill. When we see all this, we shall learn more in a year than in twenty by simply hearing you discourse and if we cannot then understand, you shall take our children, who shall be as your own. And thus being convinced that our life is a miserable one in comparison with yours, it is easy to believe that we shall adopt yours, abandoning our own.

Their words seemed to me good common sense, showing the desire they have to get a knowledge of God. It is a great wrong to let so many men be lost, and see them perish at our door, without rendering them the succor which can only be given through the help of kings, princes, and ecclesiastics, who alone have the power to do this. For to them alone belongs the honor of so great a work; namely, planting the Christian faith in an unknown region and among savage nations, since we are well informed about these people, that they long for and desire nothing so much as to be clearly instructed as to what they should do and avoid. It is accordingly the duty of those who have the power, to labor there and contribute of their abundance, for one day they must answer before God for the loss of the souls which they allowed to perish through their negligence and avarice; and these are not few but very numerous. Now this will be done when it shall please God to give them grace to this end. As for myself, I desire this result rather to-day than to-morrow, from the zeal which I have for the advancement of God's glory, for the honor of my King, and for the welfare and renown of my country.

When they are sick, the man or woman who is attacked with any disease sends for the *oqui*, who visits the patient and informs himself about the malady and the suffering. After this, the *oqui* sends for a large number of men, women, and girls, including three or four old women. These enter the cabin of the sick, dancing, each one having on his head the skin of a bear or some other wild beast, that of the bear being the most common as it is the most frightful. There are three or four other old women about the sick or suffering, who for the most part feign sickness, or are sick merely in imagination. But they are soon cured of this sickness, and generally make banquets at the expense of their friends or relatives, who give them something to put into their kettle, in addition to the presents which they receive from the dancers, such as porcelain and other bagatelles, so that they are soon cured; for when they find that they have nothing more to look for, they get up with what they have secured.

But those who are really sick are not readily cured by plays, dances, and such proceedings.

To return to my narrative: the old women near the sick person receive the presents, each singing and pausing in turn. When all the presents have been made, they proceed to lift up their voices with one accord, all singing together and keeping time with sticks on pieces of dry bark. Then all the women and girls proceed to the end of the cabin, as if they were about to begin a ballet or masquerade. The old women walk in front with their bearskins on their heads, all the others following them, one after the other. They have only two kinds of dances with regular time, one of four steps and the other of twelve, as in the *trioli* de Bretagne. They exhibit much grace in dancing. Young men often take part with them. After dancing an hour or two, the old women lead out the sick person to dance, who gets up dolefully and prepares to dance, and after a short time she dances and enjoys as much as the others. I leave it to you to consider how sick she was. Below is represented the mode of their dances.

The medicine-man thus gains honor and credit, his patient being so soon healed and on her feet. This treatment, however, does nothing for those who are dangerously ill and reduced by weakness, but causes their death rather than their cure; for I can testify that they sometimes make such a noise and hubbub from morning until two o'clock at night that it is impossible for the patient to endure it without great pain. Sometimes the patient is seized with the desire to have the women and girls dance all together, which is done in accordance with the direction of the *oqui*. But this is not all, for he and the *manitou*, accompanied by some others, make grimaces, perform magic arts, and twist themselves about so that they generally end in being out of their senses, seemingly crazy, throwing the fire from one side of the cabin to the other, eating burning coals, holding them in their hands for a while, and throwing red-hot ashes into the eyes of the spectators. Seeing them in this condition, one would say that the devil, the *oqui*, or *manitou*, if he is thus to be called, possesses and torments them. This noise and hubbub being over, they retire each to his own cabin.

But those who suffer especially during this time are the wives of those possessed, and all the inmates of their cabins, from the fear they have lest the raging ones burn up all that is in their houses. This leads them to remove everything that is in sight; for as soon as he arrives he is all in a fury, his eyes flashing and frightful, sometimes standing up, sometimes seated, as his fancy takes him. Suddenly a fit seizes him, and laying hold of everything he finds in his way he throws them to one side and the other. Then he lies down and sleeps for some time. Waking up with a jump, he seizes fire and stones which he throws about recklessly on all sides. This rage passes off with the sleep which seizes him again. Then he rages and calls several of his friends to sweat with him. The latter is the best means they have for preserving themselves in health. While they are sweating, the kettle boils to prepare them something to eat They remain, two or three hours or so, covered up with great pieces of bark and wrapped in their robes, with a great many stones about them which have been heated red hot in the fire. They sing all the time while they are in the rage, occasionally stopping to take breath. Then they give them many draughts of water to drink, since they are very thirsty, when the demoniac, who was crazy or possessed of an evil spirit, becomes sober.

Thus it happens that three or four of these sick persons get well, rather by a happy coincidence and chance than in consequence of any intelligent treatment, and this confirms their false belief that they are healed by means of these ceremonies, not considering that, for two who are thus cured, ten others die on account of the noise, great hubbub and hissing, which are rather calculated to kill than cure a sick person. But that they expect to recover their health by this noise, and we on the contrary by silence and rest, shows how the devil does everything in hostility to the good.

There are also women who go into these rages, but they do not do so much harm. They walk on all fours like beasts. Seeing this, the magician, called *oqui,* begins to sing; then, with some contortions of the face, he blows upon her, directing her to drink certain waters, and make at once a banquet of fish or flesh, which must be procured although very scarce at the time. When the shouting is over and the banquet ended, they return each to her own cabin. At another time he comes back and visits her, blowing upon her and singing in company with several others, who have been summoned for this purpose, and who hold in the hand a dry tortoise-shell filled with little pebbles, which they cause to resound in the ears of the sick woman. They direct her to make at once three or four banquets with singing and dancing, when all the girls appear adorned and painted as I have represented in figure G. The *oqui* orders masquerades, and directs them to disguise themselves, as those do who run along the streets in France on *Mardi-gras*. [196] Thus they go and sing near the bed of the sick woman and promenade through the village while the banquet is preparing to receive the maskers, who return very tired, having taken exercise enough to be able to empty the kettle of its *migan*.

According to their custom each household lives on what it gets by fishing and planting, improving as much land as it needs. They clear it up with great difficulty, since they do not have the implements adapted to this purpose. A party strip the trees of all their branches, which they burn at their base in order to kill them. They clear carefully the land between the trees, and then plant their corn at distances of a pace, putting in each place some ten kernels, and so on until they have made provision for three or four years, fearing that a bad year may befall them. The women attend to the planting and harvesting, as I have said before, and to procuring a supply of wood for winter. All the women aid each other in procuring this provision of wood, which they do in the month of March or April, in the order of two days for each. Every household is provided with as much as it needs; and if a girl marries, each woman and girl is expected to carry to the newly married one a parcel of wood for her provision, since she could not procure it alone, and at a season when she has to give her attention to other things.

The following is their mode of government: the older and leading men assemble in a council, in which they settle upon and propose all that is necessary for the affairs of the village. This is done by a plurality of voices, or in accordance with the advice of some one among them whose judgment they consider superior: such a one is requested by the company to give his opinion on the propositions that have been made, and this opinion is minutely obeyed. They have no particular chiefs with absolute command, but they show honor to the older and more courageous men, whom they name captains, as mark of honor and respect, of which there are several in a village. But, although they confer more honor upon one than upon others, yet he is not on that account to bear sway, nor esteem himself higher than his companions, unless he does so from vanity. They make no use of punishments nor arbitrary command, but accomplish everything by the entreaties of the seniors, and by means of addresses and remonstrances. Thus and not otherwise do they bring everything to pass.

They all deliberate in common, and whenever any member of the assembly offers to do anything for the welfare of the village, or to go anywhere for the service of the community, he is requested to present himself, and if he is judged capable of carrying out what he proposes, they exhort him, by fair and favorable words, to do his duty. They declare him to be an energetic man, fit for undertakings, and allure him that he will win honor in accomplishing them. In a word, they encourage him by flatteries, in order that this favorable disposition of his for the welfare of his fellow- citizens may continue and increase. Then, according to his pleasure, he refuses the responsibility, which few do, or accepts, since thereby he is held in high esteem.

When they engage in wars or go to the country of their enemies, two or three of the older or valiant captains make a beginning in the matter, and proceed to the adjoining villages to communicate their purpose, and make presents to the people of these villages, in order to induce them to accompany them to the wars in question. In so far they act as generals of armies. They designate the place where they desire to go, dispose of the prisoners who are captured, and have the direction of other matters of especial importance, of which they get the honor, if they are successful; but, if not, the disgrace of failure in the war falls upon them. These captains alone are looked upon and considered as chiefs of the tribes.

They have, moreover, general assemblies, with representatives from remote regions. These representatives come every year, one from each province, and meet in a town designated as the rendezvous of the assembly. Here are celebrated great banquets and dances, for three weeks or a month, according as they may determine. Here they renew their friendship, resolve upon and decree what they think best for the preservation of their country against their enemies, and make each other handsome presents, after which they retire each to his own district.

In burying the dead, they take the body of the deceased, wrap it in furs, and cover it very carefully with the bark of trees. Then they place it in a cabin, of the length of the body, made of bark and erected upon four posts. Others they place in the ground, propping up the earth on all sides, that it may not fall on the body, which they cover with the bark of trees, putting earth on top. Over this trench they also make a little cabin. Now it is to be understood that the bodies remain in these places, thus inhumed, but for a period of eight or ten years, when the men of the village recommend the place where their ceremonies are to take place; or, to speak more precisely, they hold a general council, in which all the people of the country are present, for the purpose of designating the place where a festival is to be held. After this they return each to his own village, where they take all the bones of the deceased, strip them and make them quite clean. These they keep very carefully, although they smell like bodies recently interred. Then all the relatives and friends of the deceased take these bones, together with their necklaces, furs, axes, kettles, and other things highly valued, and carry them, with a quantity of edibles, to the place assigned. Here, when all have assembled, they put the edibles in a place designated by the men of the village, and engage in banquets and continual dancing. The festival continues for the space of ten days, during which time other tribes, from all quarters, come to witness it and the ceremonies. The latter are attended with great outlays.

Now, by means of these ceremonies, including dances, banquets, and assemblies, as above stated, they renew their friendship to one another, saying that the bones of their relatives and friends are to be all put together, thus indicating by a figure that, as their bones are gathered together and united in one and the same place, so ought they also, during their life, to be united in one friendship and harmony, like relatives and friends, without separation. Having thus mingled together the bones of their mutual relatives and friends, they pronounce many discourses on the occasion. Then, after various grimaces or exhibitions, they make a great trench, ten fathoms square, in which they put the bones, together with the necklaces, chains of porcelain, axes, kettles, sword-blades, knives, and various other trifles, which, however, are of no slight account in their estimation. They cover the whole with earth, putting on top several great pieces of wood, and placing around many posts, on which they put a covering. This is their manner of proceeding with regard to the dead, and it is the most prominent ceremony they have. Some of them believe in the immortality of the soul, while others have only a presentiment of it, which, however, is not so very different; for they say that after their decease they will go to a place where they will sing, like crows, a song, it must be confessed, quite different from that of angels. On the following page are represented their sepulchres and manner of interment.

It remains to describe how they spend their time in winter; namely, from the month of December to the end of March, or the beginning of our spring, when the snow melts. All that they might do during autumn, as I have before stated, they postpone to be done during winter; namely, their banquetings, and usual dances for the sake of the sick, which I have already described, and the assemblages of the inhabitants of various villages, where there are banquetings, singing, and dances, which they call *tabagies* [197] and where sometimes five hundred persons are collected, both men, women, and girls. The latter are finely decked and adorned with the best and most costly things they have.

On certain days they make masquerades, and visit each other's cabins, asking for the things they like, and if they meet those who have what they want, these give it to them freely. Thus they go on asking for many things without end; so that a single one of those soliciting will have robes of beaver, bear, deer, lynxes, and other furs, also fish, Indian corn, tobacco, or boilers, kettles, pots, axes, pruning-knives, knives, and other like things. They go to the houses and cabins of the village, singing these words, That one gave me this, another gave that, or like words, by way of commendation. But if one gives them nothing they get angry, and show such spite towards him that when they leave they take a stone and put it near this man or that woman who has not given them anything. Then, without saying a word, they return singing, which is a mark of insult, censure, and ill-will. The women do so as well as the men, and this mode of proceeding takes place at night, and the masquerade continues seven or eight days. There are some of their villages which have maskers or merry-makers, as we do on the evening of *Mardi-gras*, and they invite the other villages to come and see them and win their utensils, if they can. Meanwhile banquets are not wanting. This is the way they spend their time in winter.

Moreover the women spin, and pound meal for the journeys of their husbands in summer, who go to other tribes to trade, as they decide to do at the above-mentioned councils, in which it is determined what number of men may go from each village, that it may not be deprived of men of war for its protection; and nobody goes from the country without the general consent of the chiefs, or if they should go they would be regarded as behaving improperly. The men make nets for fishing, which they carry on in summer, but generally in winter, when they capture the fish under the ice with the line or with the seine.

The following is their manner of fishing. They make several holes in a circular form in the ice, the one where they are to draw the seine being some five feet long and three wide. Then they proceed to place their net at this opening, attaching it to a rod of wood from six to seven feet long, which they put under the ice. This rod they cause to pass from hole to hole, when one or more men, putting their hands in the holes, take hold of the rod to which is attached an end of the net, until they unite at the opening of five to six feet. Then they let the net drop to the bottom of the water, it being sunk by little stones attached to the end. After it is down they draw it up again with their arms at its two ends, thus capturing the fish that are in it. This is, in brief, their manner of fishing in winter.

The winter begins in the month of November and continues until the month of
April, when the trees begin to send forth the sap and show their buds.

On the 22d of the month of April we received news from our interpreter, who had gone to Carantoüan, through those who had come from there. They told us that they had left him on the road, he having returned to the village for certain reasons.

Now, resuming the thread of my narrative, our savages assembled to come with us, and conduct us back to our habitation, and for this purpose we set out from their country on the 20th of the month, [198] and were forty days on the way. We caught a large number of fish and animals of various kinds, together with small game, which afforded us especial pleasure, in addition to the provisions thus furnished us for our journey. Upon our arrival among the French, towards the end of the month of June, I found Sieur du Pont Gravé, who had come from France with two vessels, and who had almost despaired of seeing me again, having heard from the savages the bad news, that I was dead.

We also saw all the holy fathers who had remained at our settlement. They too were very happy to see us again, and we none the less so to see them. Welcomes, and felicitations on all sides being over, I made arrangements to set out from, the Falls of St. Louis for our settlement, taking with me my host D'Arontal. I took leave also of all the other savages, assuring them of my affection, and that, if I could, I would see them in the suture, to assist them as I had already done in the past, bringing them valuable presents to secure their friendship with one another, and begging them to forget all the disputes which they had had when I reconciled them, which they promised to do.

Then we set out, on the 8th of July, and arrived at our settlement on the 11th of that month. Here I found everybody in good health, and we all, in company with our holy fathers, who chanted the Divine service, returned thanks to God for His care in preserving us, and protecting us amid the many perils and dangers to which we had been exposed.

After this, and when everything had become settled, I proceeded to show hospitalities to my host, D'Arontal, who admired our building, our conduct, and mode of living. After carefully observing us, he said to me, in private, that he should never die contented until he had seen all of his friends, or at least a good part of them, come and take up their abode with us, in order to learn how to serve God, and our way of living, which he esteemed supremely happy in comparison with their own. Moreover he said that, if he could not learn it by word of mouth, he would do so much better and more easily by sight and by frequent intercourse, and that, if their minds could not comprehend our arts, sciences, and trades, their children who were young could do so, as they had often represented to us in their country in conversation with Father Joseph. He urged us, for the promotion of this object, to make another settlement at the Falls of St. Louis, so as to secure them the passage of the river against their enemies, assuring us that, as soon as we should build a house, they would come in numbers to live as brothers with us. Accordingly I promised to make a settlement for them as soon as possible.

After we had remained four or five days together, I gave him some valuable presents, with which he was greatly pleased, and I begged him to continue his affection for us, and come again to see our settlement with his friends. Then he returned happy to the Falls of St Louis, where his companions awaited him.

When this Captain D'Arontal had departed, we enlarged our habitation by a third at least in buildings and fortifications, since it was not sufficiently spacious, nor convenient for receiving the members of our own company and likewise the strangers that might come to see us. We used, in building, lime and sand entirely, which we found very good there in a spot near the habitation. This is a very useful material for building for those disposed to adapt and accustom themselves to it.

The Fathers Denis and Joseph determined to return to France, in order to testify there to all they had seen, and to the hope they could promise themselves of the conversion of these people, who awaited only the assistance of the holy fathers in order to be converted and brought to our faith and the Catholic religion.

During my stay at the settlement I had some common grain cut; namely, French grain, which had been planted there and which had come up very finely, that I might take it to France, as evidence that the land is good and fertile. In another part, moreover, there was some fine Indian corn, also scions and trees which had been given us by Sieur du Monts in Normandy. In a word all the gardens of the place were in an admirably fine condition, being planted with peas, beans, and other vegetables, also squashes, and very superior radishes of various sorts, cabbages, beets, and other kitchen vegetables. When on the point of departure, we left two of our fathers at the settlement; namely, Fathers Jean d'Olbeau and Pacifique, [199] who were greatly pleased with all the time spent at that place, and resolved to await there the return of Father Joseph, [200] who was expected to come back in the following year, which he did.

We sailed in our barques the 20th day of July, and arrived at Tadoussac the 23d day of the month, where Sieur du Pont Gravé awaited us with his vessel ready and equipped. In this we embarked and set out the 3d day of the month of August. The wind was so favorable that we arrived in health by the grace of God, at Honfleur, on the 10th day of September, one thousand six hundred and sixteen, and upon our arrival rendered praise and thanks to God for his great care in preserving our lives, and delivering and even snatching us, as it were, from the many dangers to which we had been exposed, and for bringing and conducting us in health to our country; we besought Him also to move the heart of our King, and the gentlemen of his council, to contribute their assistance so far as necessary to bring these poor savages to the knowledge of God, whence honor will redound to his Majesty, grandeur and growth to his realm, profit to his subjects, and the glory of all these undertakings and toils to God, the sole author of all excellence, to whom be honor and glory. Amen.

ENDNOTES:

78. Champlain's first voyage was made in 1603, and this journal was published in 1619. It was therefore fully fifteen years since his explorations began.

79. *Vide Histoire du Canada,* par Sagard, Trois ed., pp 27, 28. The reader is likewise referred to the Memoir of Champlain, Vol. I. pp 122-124.

80. Bernard du Verger, a man of exalted virtue—*Laverdière.*

81. Robert Ubaldim was nuncio at this time. *Vide Laverdière in loco.*

82. Denis Jamay. Sagard writes this name *Jamet.*

83. Jean d'Olbeau. *Vide Histoire du Canada,* par Gabriel Sagard, Paris, 1636, Tross ed., Vol. I. p. 28.

84. Pacifique du Plessis was a lay-brother, although the title of Father is

given to him by several early writers. *Vide citations by Laverdière in loco,* Quebec ed., Vol. IV. p. 7.

85. Read April 24. It is obvious from the context that it could not be August. Sagard says *le 24 d'Auril. Vide Histoire du Canada,* Trois ed., Vol. I. p 36.

86. The Recollect Father Joseph le Caron.

87. *Vide Laverdière in loco.*

88. Father Denis Jamay.

89. Jean d'Olbeau and Pacifique du Plessis.

90. This refers to the volume bearing date 1613, but which may not have
been actually issued from the press till 1614.

91. Our views of the war policy of Champlain are stated at some length in
Vol I. pp 189-193.

92. Laverdière thinks it probable that Champlain left the Falls of St Louis on the 23d of June, and that the Holy Mass was celebrated on the Rivière des Prairies on the 24th, the festival of St John the Baptist.

93. This interpreter was undoubtedly Etienne Brûlé. It was a clearly defined policy of Champlain to send suitable young men among the savages, particularly to learn their language, and subsequently to act as interpreters. Brûlé is supposed to have been of this class.

94. The Lake of Two Mountains.

95. The River Ottawa, which Champlain had explored in 1613, as far as Allumet Island, where a tribe of the Algonquins resided, called later *Kichesipinni. Vide Relation des Jésuites,* 1640, p 34.

96. This is an over-estimate.

97. Champlain here again, *Vide* note 90, refers to the issue bearing date 1613. It is not unlikely that while it bears the imprint of 1613, it did not actually issue from the press till 1614.

98. The lake or expansion of the Ottawa on the southern side of Allumet Island was called the lake of the Algonquins, as Allumet Island was oftentimes called the Island of the Algonquins.

99. The River Ottawa.

100. Père Vimont calls this tribe *Kotakoutouemi. Relation des Jésuites,* 1640, p. 34. Père Rogueneau gives *Outaoukotouemiouek,* and remarks that their language is a mixture of Algonquin and Montagnais. *Vide Relation des Jésuites,* 1650. p. 34; also *Laverdière in loco.*

101. *Blues,* blueberries. The Canada blueberry. *Vaccinium Canadense.* Under the term *blues* several varieties may have been included. Charlevoix describes and figures this fruit under the name _Bluet du Canada. *Vide Description des Plantes Principales de l'Amérique Septentrionale,* in *Histoire de la Nouvelle France,* Paris. 1744, Tom. IV. pp. 371, 372; also Vol. I: p 303, note 75, of this work.

102. At its junction with the Mattawan, the Ottawa's course is from the north. What is known as its east branch rises 150 miles north of the city of Ottawa. Extending towards the west in a winding course for the distance of about 300 miles, it turns towards the southeast, and a few miles before it joins the Mattawan its course is directly south. From its northeastern source by a short portage is reached the river Chomouchouan, an affluent of Lake St. John and the Saguenay.

103. Mattawa is 197 miles from Ottawa. We have no means of giving the latitude with entire accuracy, but it is about 46° 20'.

104. Lac du Talon and Lac la Tortue.

105. Nipissings, or Nipissirini. Champlain writes *Nipisierinii.*

106. On the 26th of July, The distance from the junction of the Ottawa and the Mattawan to Lake Nipissing is about thirty-two miles If *lieues* were translated miles, it would be a not very incorrect estimate.

107. *Vide* the representations here referred to.

108. Lake Nipissing, whose dimensions are over-stated.

109. Sturgeon River.

110. Père Vimont gives the names of these tribes as follows,—*Timiscimi, Outimagami, Ouachegami, Mitchitamou, Outurbi, Kiristinon. Vide Relation des Jésuites.* 1640. p. 34.

111. French River.

112. *Blues. Vide antea,* note 101.

113. This significant name is given with reference to their mode of dressing their hair.

114. Blueberries, *Vaccinium Canadense.*

115. *De cuir beullu,* for *cúir bouilli,* literally "boiled leather."

116. The shields of the savages of this region may have been made of the hide of the buffalo, although the range of this animal was far to the northwest of them. Champlain saw undoubtedly among the Hurons skins of the buffalo. *Vide postea,* note 180.

117. Lake Huron is here referred to.

118. The greatest length of Lake Huron on a curvilinear line, between the discharge of St Mary's Strait and the outlet, is about 240 miles; its length due north and south is 186 miles, and its extreme breadth about 220 miles. *Bouchette.*

119. Coasting along the eastern shore of the Georgian Bay, when they arrived at Matchedash Bay they crossed it in a southwesterly course and entered the country of the Attigouautans, or, as they are sometimes called, the Attignaouentans. *Relation des Jésuites,* 1640, p. 78. They were a principal tribe of the Hurons, living within the limits of the present county of Simcoe. It is to be regretted that the Jesuit Fathers did not accompany their relations with local maps by

which we could fix, at least approximately, the Indian towns which they visited, and with which they were so familiar. For a description of the Hurons and of their country, the origin of the name and other interesting particulars, *vide Pere Hierosine Lalemant, Relation des Jésuites*, 1639, Quebec ed. p. 50.

120. *Sitrouilles* for *citrouilles*. *Vide* Vol II. p. 64, note 128.

121. *Herbe au soleil*. The sunflower of Northeast America, *Helianthus multiflorus*. This species is found from Quebec to the Saskatchewan, a tributary of Lake Winnipeg. *Vide Chronological History of Plants*, by Charles Pickering, M.D., Boston, 1879. p. 914. Charlevoix, in the description of his journey through Canada in 1720, says: "The Soleil is a plant very common in the fields of the savages, and which grows seven or eight feet high. Its flower, which is very large, is in the shape of the marigold, and the seed grows in the same manner. The savages, by boiling it, draw out an oil, with which they grease their hair." *Letters to the Dutchess of Lesdiguieres*, London, 1763, p. 95.

122. *Vignes* Probably the frost grape, *Vitis cordifolia*.

123. *Prunes*. The Canada plum, *Prunus Americana*.

124. *Framboises*. The wild red raspberry, *Rubus strigosus*.

125. *Fraises*. The wild strawberry, *Fragaria Virginiana*. *Vide Pickering Chro. Hist. Plants*, p. 771.

126. *Petites pommes sauuages*. Probably the American crab-apple, *Pyrus coronaria*.

127. *Noix* This may include the butternut and some varieties of the walnut. *Vide* Vol. I. p. 264.

128. Doubtless the May-apple, *Podophyllum peltatum*. In the wilds of Simcoe this fruit may have seemed tolerable from the absence of others more desirable. Gray says, "It is slightly acid, mawkish, eaten by pigs and boys." *Cf. Florula Bostioniensis*, by Jacob Bigelow, M.D. Boston, 1824, pp. 215, 216.

129. *Les Chesnes, ormeaux, & heslres*. For oaks see Vol I. p. 264. Elms, plainly the white elm, *Ulmus Americana*, so called in contradistinction to the red or slippery elm, *Ulmus fulva*. The savages sometimes used the bark of the slippery elm in the construction of their canoes when the white birch could not be obtained. *Vide Charlevoix's Letters*, 1763, p. 94. For the beech, see Vol. I. p. 264.

130. *Perdrix*. Canada Grouse, *Tetrao Canadensis*, sometimes called the Spruce Partridge, differing from the partridge of New England, which is the Ruffed Grouse, *Bonasa umbellus*. This latter species is, however, found likewise in Canada.

131. *Lapins*. The American hare, *Lepus Americanus*.

132. *Cerises petites*. Reference is evidently here made to the wild red cherry, *Prunus Pennsylvanica*, which is the smallest of all the native species. *Cf.* Vol. I. p. 264.

133. *Merises*. The wild black cherry, *Prunus serotina*.

134. The Carantouanais. *Vide Carte de la Nouvelle France*, 1632, *also* Vol. I. p. 304. This tribe was probably situated on the upper waters of the Susquehanna, and consequently south of the Five Nations, although we said inadvertently in Vol. I. p. 128 that they were on the west of them. General John S. Clark thinks their village was at Waverly, near the border of Pennsylvania In Vol. I. p. 143. in the 13th line from the top, we should have said the Carantouanais instead of *Entouhonorons*.

135. The Entouhonorons were a part, it appears, of the Five Nations. Champlain says they unite with the Iroquois in making war against all the other tribes except the Neutral Nation. Lake Ontario is called *Lac des Entouhonorons*, and Champlain adds that their country is near the River St. Lawrence, the passage of which they forbid to all other tribes. *Vide* Vol. I. pp. 303, 304. He thus appears to apply the name *Iroquois* to the eastern portion of the Five Nations, particularly those whom he had attacked on Lake Champlain; and the Huron name, *Entouhonorons*, to the western portion. The subdivisions, by which they were distinguished at a later period, were probably not then known, at least not to Champlain.

136. *Flamens*. The Dutch were at this time on the Hudson, qengaged in the fur trade with the savages. *Vide History of the State of*

New York by John Romeyn Brodhead, New York, 1853. pp. 38-65. *History of New Netherland* or *New York under the Dutch*, by E. B. O'Callaghan, New York, 1846, pp. 67-77.

137. Their enemies were the Iroquois.

138. *Chouontouaroüon*, another name for *Entouhoronon*.

139. Lake Couchiching, a small sheet of water into which pass by a small outlet the waters of Lake Simcoe.

140. Lake Simcoe. Laverdière says the Indian name of this lake was *Ouentaronk*, and that it was likewise called *Lac aux Claies*.

141. Étienne Brûlé. *Vide postea*, p. 208.

142. *Dans ces lacs*. From Lake Chouchiching, coasting along the northeastern shore of Lake Simcoe, they would make five or six leagues in reaching a point nearest to Sturgeon Lake.

143. Undoubtedly Sturgeon Lake.

144. From their entrance of Sturgeon Lake to the point where they reached Lake Ontario, at the eastern limit of Amherst Island, the distance is, in its winding and circuitous course, not far from Champlain's estimate, viz. sixty-four leagues. That part of the river above Rice Lake is the Otonabee; that below is known as the Trent.

145. *Gruës* The white crane, *Grus Americanus* Adult plumage pure white *Coues's Key to North American Birds*, Boston, 1872, p 271 Charlevoix says, "We have cranes of two colors, some white and others *gris de lin*," that is a purple or lilac color. This latter species is the brown crane, *Grus Canadensis*. "Plumage plumbeous gray." *Coues*. *Vide Charlevoix's Letters*, London. 1763, p 83.

146. The latitude of the eastern end of Amherst Island is about 44° 11'.

147. This traverse, it may be presumed, was made by coasting along the shore, as was the custom of the savages with their light canoes.

148. It appears that, after making by estimate about fourteen leagues in their bark canoes, and four by land along the shore, they struck inland. Guided merely by the distances given in the text, it is not possible to determine with exactness at what point they left the lake. This arises from the fact that we are not sure at what point the measurement began, and the estimated distances are given, moreover, with very liberal margins. But the eighteen leagues in all would take them not very far from Little Salmon River, whether the estimate were made from the eastern end of Amherst Island or Simcoe Island, or any place in that immediate neighborhood. The natural features of the country, for four leagues along the coast north of Little Salmon River, answer well to the description given in the text. The chestnut and wild grape are still found there. *Vide MS. Letters of the Rev. James Cross, D.D., LL.D., and of S.Z. Smith, Esq.*, of Mexico, New York.

149. Lake Ontario, or Lake of the Entouhonorons, is about a hundred and eighty miles long, and about fifty-five miles in its extreme width.

150. The river here crossed was plainly Oneida River, flowing from Oneida Lake into Lake Ontario. The lake is identified by the islands in it. Oneida Lake is the only one in this region which contains any islands whatever, and consequently the river flowing from it must be that now known as Oneida River.

151. For the probable site of this fort, see Vol. I. p. 130, note 83.

152. They were of the tribe called Carantouanais. *Vide antea*, note 134.

153. This was in the month of October.

154. *Et après auoir trauersé le bout du lac de laditte isle*. From this form of expression this island would seem to have been visited before. But no particular island is mentioned on their former traverse of the lake. It is impossible to fix with certainty upon the isiand referred to. It may have been Simcoe or Wolf Island, or some other.

155. Probably Cataraqui Creek. *Vide* Vol. I. p. 136.

156. Perhaps Loughborough Lake, or the system of lakes of which this is a part.

157. *Cygnes*, swans. Probably the Trumpeter Swan, *Cygnus buccinator*. They were especially found in Sagard's time about Lake Nipissing. "Mais pour des Cignes, qu'ils appellent *Horhev*, il y en a principalement vers les Epicerinys." *Vide Le Grand Voyage av Pays des Hurons* par Fr. Gabriel Sagard, Paris, 1632, p. 303.

158. *Gruës blanches. Vide antea*, n. 145.

159. *Houstardes. Vide antea*, note 32.

160. *Mauuis*, Song-Thrush. Doubtless the Robin, *Turdus migratorius*.

161. *Allouettes*, larks. Probably the Brown Lark, *Anthus ludovicianus*. Found everywhere in North America.

162. *Beccassines*. Probably the American Snipe, *Gallinago Wilsonii*.

163. *Oyes*, geese. The common Wild Goose, *Branta Canadensis*, or it may include all the species taken collectively. For the several species found in Canada, *vide antea*, note 32.

164. *Les loups*. The American Wolf, *Lupus occidentalis*.

165. The thirty-eight days during which they were there would include the whole period from the time they began to make their preparations on the 28th of October on the shores of Lake Ontario till they began their homeward journey on the 4th of December. *Vide antea*, p. 137; *postea*, p. 143.

166. The author here refers to the chief D'Arontal, whose guest he was. *Vide antea*, 137. Cf. also Quebec ed. 1632, p. 928.

167. *Trainees de bois*, a kind of sledge. The Indian's sledge was made of two pieces of board, which, with his stone axe and perhaps with the aid of fire, he patiently manufactured from the trunks of trees. The boards were each about six inches wide and six or seven feet long, curved upward at the forward end and bound together by cross pieces. The sides were bordered with strips of wood, which served as brackets, to which was fastened the strap that bound the baggage upon the sledge. The load was dragged by a rope or strap of leather passing round the breast of the savage and attached to the end of the sledge. The sledge was so narrow that it could be drawn easily and without impediment wherever the savage could thread his way through the pathless forests.

The journey from their encampment northeast of Kingston on Lake Ontario to the capital of the Hurons was not less in a straight line than a hundred and sixty miles. Without a pathway, in the heart of winter, through water and melting snow, with their heavy burdens, the hardship and exhaustion can hardly be exaggerated.

168. Namely at Cahiagué. In the issue of 1632, Champlain says they arrived on the 23d day of the month. *Vide* Quebec ed, p. 929. Leaving on the 4th and travelling nineteen days, as stated above, they would arrive on the 23d December.

169. Probably the 4th of January.

170. Father Joseph Le Caron had remained at Carhagouha, during the absence of the war party in their attack upon the Iroquois, where Champlain probably arrived on the 5th of January.

171. In the issue of 1632, the arrival of Champlain and Le Caron is stated to have occurred on the 17th of January. This harmonizes with the correction of dates in notes 169, 170.

The Huron name of the Petuns was *Tionnontateronons*, or *Khionontateronons*, or *Quieunontateronons*. Of them Vimont says, "Les Khionontateronons, qu'on appelle la nation du Petun, pour l'abondance qu'il y a de cette herbe, sont eloignez du pays des Hurons, dont ils parlent la langue, enuiron douze ou quinze lieues tirant à l'Occident." *Vide Relation des Jésuites*, 1640, p. 95; *His. Du Canada*, Vol. I. p. 209. Sagard.

For some account of the subsequent history of the Nation de Petun, *vide Indian Migration in Ohio*, by C. C. Baldwin, 1879, p. 2.

172. It was of great importance to the Indians to select a site for their villages where suitable wood was accessible, both for fortifying them with palisades and for fuel in the winter. It could not be brought a great distance for either of these purposes. Hence when the wood in the vicinity became exhausted they were compelled to remove and build anew.

173. That is to say like the Hurons.

174. The Nation Neutre was called by the Hurons *Attisandaronk* or *Attihouandaron. Vide Relation des Jésuites*, 1641, p. 72; *Dictonaire de la Langue Huronne,* par Sagard, a Paris, 1632. Champlain places them, on his map of 1632, south of Lake Erie. His knowledge of that lake, obtained from the savages, was very meagre as the map itself shows. The Neutres are placed by early writers on the west of Lake Ontario and north of Lake Erie *Vide Laverdière in loco,* Quebec ed., p. 546; also, *Indian Migration in Ohio,* by C. C. Baldwin, p. 4. They are placed far to the south of Lake Erie by Nicholas Sanson. *Vide Cartes de l'Amerique,* 1657.

175. The Cheveux Relevés are represented by Champlain as dwelling west of the Petuns, and were probably not far from the most southern limit of the Georgian Bay. Strangely enough Nicholas Sanson places them on a large island that separates the Georgian Bay from Lake Huron. *Vide Cartes de l'Amerique* par N. Sanson, 1657.

176. *Atsistaehronons, ou Nation du Feu*. Their Algonquin name was Mascoutins or Maskoutens. with several other orthographies. The significance of their name is given by Sagard as follows: Ils sont errans, sinon que quelques villages d'entr'eux fement des bleds d'Inde, et font la guerre à vne autre Nation, nommée *Assitagueronon,* qui veut dire gens de feu: car en langue Huronne *Assista* signifie du feu, et *Eronon,* signifie Nation. *Le Grand Voyage du Pays des Hurons,* par Gabriel Sagard, a Paris, 1632, p. 78. *Vide Relation des Jésuites,* 1641, p 72; *Discovery and Exploration of the Mississippi Valley,* by John Gilmary Shea, p. 13; *Indian Migration in Ohio,* by C. C. Baldwin, pp 9, 10; Discovery of the *Northwest by John Nicolet,* by C. W. Butterfield, p. 63; *L'Amerique en Plusieurs Cartes,* par N. Sanson, 1657.

177. *Pisierinii,* the Nipissings. This relates to those Nipissings who had accompanied Champlain on the expedition against the Iroquois, and who were passing the winter among the Hurons. He had

expected that they would accompany him on explorations on the north of them. But arriving at their encampment, on his return from the Petuns and Cheveux Relevés, he learned from them of the quarrel that had arisen between the Algonquins and the Hurons.

178. Attigouantans, the principal tribe of the Hurons.

179. *Colliers de pourceline.* These necklaces were composed of shells, pierced and strung like beads. They were of a violet color, and were esteemed of great value. The *branches* were strings of white shells, and were more common and less valuable. An engraved representation may be seen in *Histoire de L'Amérique Septentrionale,* par De la Potherie, Paris, 1722, Tom. I. p. 334. For a full description of these necklaces and their significance and use in their councils, *vide Charlevoix's Letters,* London, 1763, p 132.

180. *Buffles,* buffaloes. The American Bison, *Bos Americanus.* The skins seen by Champlain in the possession of the savages seem to indicate that the range of the buffalo was probably further east at that period than at the present time, its eastern limit being now about the Red River, which flows into Lake Winnipeg. The limit of its northern range is generally stated to be at latitude 60 degrees, but it is sometimes found as far north as 63 degrees or 64 degrees. *Vide* Dr. Shea's interesting account of the buffalo in *Discovery and Exploration of Mississippi Valley,* p. 18. The range of the Musk Ox is still farther north, rarely south of latitude 67 degrees. His home is in the Barren Grounds, west of Hudson Bay, and on the islands on the north of the American Continent, where he subsists largely on lichens and the meagre herbage of that frosty region.

181. Champlain is here speaking of the whole country of New France.

182. This sentence in the original is unfinished and defective. *Au costé vers le Nort, icelle grande riuiere terant à l'Occident, etc.* In the ed. 1632, the reading is *Au costé vers le nort d'icelle grande riuiere tirant au suroust, etc.* The tranlation is according to the ed. of 1632. *Vide* Quebec ed., p. 941.

183. Champlain here gives the four species of the *cervus* family under names then known to him, viz, the moose, wapiti or elk, caribou, and the common deer.

184. *Fouines*, a quadruped known as the minx or mink, *Mustela vison*.

185. *Martes*, weasels, *Mustela vulgaris*.

186. *The country on the north*, &c. Having described the country along the coast of the St Lawrence and the lakes he now refers to the country still further north even to the southern borders of Hudson's Bay *Vide* small map.

187. *Almouchiquois*, so in the French for Almouchiquois. All the tribes at and south of *Chouacoet*, or the mouth of the Saco River, were denominated Almouchiquois by the French. *Vide* Vol II p 63, *et passim*.

188. The country of the Attigouantans, sometimes written Attigouautans, the principal tribe of the Hurons, used by Champlain as including the whole, with whom the French were in close alliance, was from east to west not more than about twelve leagues. There must have been some error by which the author is made to say that it was *two hundred and thirty leagues*. Laverdière suggests that in the manuscript it might have been 23, or 20 to 30, and that the printer made it 230.

189. The author plainly means that the country of the Hurons was nearly surrounded by the Mer Douce; that is to say, by Lake Huron and the waters connected with it, viz., the River Severn, Lake Couchiching, and Lake Simcoe. As to the population, compare *The Jesuits in North America*, by Francis Parkman, LL.D., note p. xxv.

190. *Vide antea*, note 172, for the reason of these removals.

191. *Febues du Brésil*. This was undoubtedly the common trailing bean, *Pliaseolus vulgaris*, probably called the Brazilian bean, because it resembled a bean known under that name. It was found in cultivation in New England as mentioned by Champlain and the early English settlers. Bradford discoursing of the Indians, *His. Plymouth Plantation*, p. 83, speaks of "their beans of various collours." It is

possible that the name, *febues du Brésil*, was given to it on account of its red color, as was that of the Brazil-wood, from the Portuguese word *braza*, a burning coal.

192. *Vide antea*, note 101.

193. *Sitrouelles*, or *citrouilles*, the common summer squash, *Cucurbita polymorpha. Vide* Vol. II. note 128. For figure D, *vide* p. 116.

194. The coloring matter appears to have been derived from the root of the bedstraw, *Galium tinctorum*. Peter Kalm, a pupil of Linnæus, who travelled in Canada in 1749, says, "The roots of this plant are employed by the Indians in dyeing the quills of the American porcupines red, which they put into several pieces of their work, and air, sun, or water seldom change this color." *Travels into North America*, London, 1771, Vol. III. pp. 14-15.

195. Père Joseph Le Caron, who had passed the winter among the Hurons.

196. *Mardi-gras*, Shrove-Tuesday, or *flesh Tuesday*, the last day of the Carnival, the day before Ash Wednesday, the first day in Lent.

197. *Vide* Vol. I. pp. 236-238.

198. This must have been on the 20th of May.

199. Jean d'Olbeau and the lay brother Pacifique du Plessis.

200. Joseph le Caron, who accompanied Champlain to France.

CONTINUATION OF THE VOYAGES AND DISCOVERIES MADE IN NEW FRANCE, BY SIEUR DE CHAMPLAIN, CAPTAIN FOR THE KING IN THE WESTERN MARINE, IN THE YEAR 1618.

At the beginning of the year one thousand six hundred and eighteen, on the twenty-second of March, I set out from Paris, [201] together with my brother-in-law, [202] for Honfleur, our usual port of embarkation. There we were obliged to make a long stay on account of contrary winds. But when they had become favorable, we embarked on the large vessel of the association, which Sieur du Pont Gravé commanded. There was also on board a nobleman, named De la Mothe, [203] who had previously made a voyage with the Jesuits to the regions of La Cadie, where he was taken prisoner by the English, and by them carried to the Virginias, the place of their settlement. Some time after they transferred him to England and from there to France, where there arose in him an increased desire to make another voyage to New France, which led him to seek the opportunity presented by me. I had assured him, accordingly, that I would use my influence and assistance with our associates, as it seemed to me that they would find such a person desirable, since he would be very useful in those regions.

Our embarkation being made, we took our departure from Honfleur on the 24th day of May following, in the year 1618. The wind was favorable for our voyage, but continued so only a very few days, when it suddenly changed, and we had all the time head winds up to our arrival, on the 3d day of June following, on the Grand Bank, where the fresh fishery is carried on. Here we perceived to the windward of us some banks of ice, which came down from the north. While waiting for a favorable wind we engaged in fishing, which afforded us great pleasure, not only on account of the fish but also of a kind of bird called *fauquets*, [204] and other kinds that are caught on the line like fish. For, on throwing the line, with its hook baited with cod liver, these birds made for it with a rush, and in such numbers that you could not draw it out in order to throw it again, without capturing them by the beak, feet, and wings as they slew and fell upon the bait, so great were the eagerness and voracity of these birds. This fishing afforded us great pleasure, not only on account of the sport, but on account of the infinite number of birds and fish that we captured, which were very good eating, and made a very desirable change on shipboard.

Continuing on our route, we arrived on the 15th of the month off Isle Percée, and on St. John's day [205] following entered the harbor of Tadoussac, where we found our small vessel, which had arrived three weeks before us. The men on her told us that Sieur des Chesnes, the commander, had gone to our settlement at Quebec. Thence he was to go to the Trois Rivières to meet the savages, who were to come there from various regions for the purpose of trade, and likewise to determine what was to be done on account of the death of two of our men, who had been treacherously and perfidiously killed by two vicious young men of the Montagnais. These two unfortunate victims, as the men on the vessel informed us, had been killed while out hunting nearly two years [206] before. Those in the settlement had always supposed that they had been drowned from the upsetting of their canoe, until a short time before, one of the men, conceiving an animosity against the murderers, made a disclosure and communicated the fact and cause of the murder to the men of our settlement. For certain reasons it has seemed to me well to give an account of the matter and of what was done in regard to it. But it is almost impossible to obtain the exact truth in the case, on account, not only of the small amount of testimony at hand, but of the diversity of the statements made, the most of which were presumptive. I will, however, give an account of the matter here, following the statement of the greater number as being nearer the truth, and relating what I have found to be the most probable.

The following is the occasion of the murder of the two unfortunate deceased. One of the two murderers paid frequent visits to our settlement, receiving there a thousand kindnesses and favors, among other persons from Sieur du Parc, a nobleman from Normandy, in command at the time at Quebec, in the service of the King and in behalf of the merchants of the Association in the year 1616. This savage, while on one of his customary visits, received one day, on account of some jealousy, ill treatment from one of the two murdered men, who was by profession a locksmith, and who after some words beat the savage so soundly as to impress it well upon his memory. And not satisfied with beating and misusing the savage he incited his companions to do the same, which aroused still more the hatred and animosity of the savage towards this locksmith and his companions, and led him to seek an opportunity to revenge himself. He accordingly watched for a time and opportunity for doing so, acting however cautiously and appearing as usual, without showing any sign of resentment.

Some time after, the locksmith and a sailor named Charles Pillet, from the island of Ré, arranged to go hunting and stay away three or four nights. For this purpose they got ready a canoe, and embarking departed from Quebec for Cape Tourmente. Here there were some little islands where a great quantity of game and birds resorted, near Isle d'Orleans, and distant seven leagues from Quebec. The departure of our men became at once known to the two savages, who were not slow in starting to pursue them and carry out their evil design. They sought for the place where the locksmith and his companion went to sleep, in order to surprise them. Having ascertained it at evening, at break of day on the following morning, the two savages slipped quietly along certain very pleasant meadows. Arriving at a point near the place in question, they moored their canoe, landed and went straight to the cabin, where our men had slept. But they found only the locksmith, who was preparing to go hunting with his companion, and who thought of nothing less than of what was to befall him. One of these savages approached him, and with some pleasant words removed from him all suspicion of anything wrong in order that he might the better deceive him. But as he saw him stoop to adjust his arquebus, he quickly drew a club that he had concealed on his person, and gave the locksmith so heavy a blow on his head, that it sent him staggering and completely stunned. The savage, seeing that the locksmith was preparing to defend himself, repeated his blow, struck him to the ground, threw himself upon him, and with a knife gave him three or four cuts in the stomach, killing him in this horrible manner.

In order that they might also get possession of the sailor, the companion of the locksmith who had started early in the morning to go hunting, not because they bore any special hatred towards him, but that they might not be discovered nor accused by him, they went in all directions searching for him. At last, from the report of an arquebus which they heard, they discovered where he was, in which direction they rapidly hastened, so as to give no time to the sailor to reload his arquebus and put himself in a state of defence. Approaching, they fired their arrows at him, by which having prostrated him, they ran upon him and finished him with the knife.

Then the assassins carried off the body, together with the other, and, binding them so firmly together that they would not come apart, attached to them a quantity of stones and pebbles, together with their weapons and clothes, so as not to be discovered by any sign, after which they carried them to the middle of the river, threw them in, and they sank to the bottom. Here they remained a long time until, through the will of God, the cords broke, and the bodies were washed ashore and thrown far up on the bank, to serve as accusers and incontestable witnesses of the attack of these two cruel and treacherous assassins. For the two bodies were found at a distance of more than twenty feet from the water in the woods, but had not become separated in so long a time, being still firmly bound, the bones, stripped of the flesh like a skeleton, alone remaining. For the two victims, contrary to the expectation of the two murderers, who thought they had done their work so secretly that it would never be known, were found a long time after their disappearance by the men of our settlement, who, pained at their absence, searched for them along the banks of the river. But God in his justice would not permit so enormous a crime, and had caused it to be exposed by another savage, their companion, in retaliation for an injury he had received from them. Thus their wicked acts were disclosed.

The holy Fathers and the men of the settlement were greatly surprised at seeing the bodies of these two unfortunates, with their bones all bare, and their skulls broken by the blows received from the club of the savages. The Fathers and others at the settlement advised to preserve them in some portion of the settlement until the return of our vessels, in order to consult with all the French as to the best course to pursue in the matter. Meanwhile our people at the settlement resolved to be on their guard, and no longer allow so much freedom to these savages as they had been accustomed to, but on the contrary require reparation for so cruel a murder by a process of justice, or some other way, or let things in the mean time remain as they were, in order the better to await our vessels and our return, that we might all together consult what was to be done in the matter.

But the savages seeing that this iniquity was discovered, and that they and the murderer were obnoxious to the French, were seized with despair, and, fearing that our men would exercise vengeance upon them for this murder, withdrew for a while from our settlement.[207] Not only those guilty of the act but the others also being seized with fear came no longer to the settlement, as they had been accustomed to do, but waited for greater security for themselves.

Finding themselves deprived of intercourse with us, and of their usual welcome, the savages sent one of their companions named by the French, *La Ferrière*, to make their excuses for this murder; namely, they asserted they had never been accomplices in it, and had never consented to it, and that, if it was desired to have the two murderers for the sake of inflicting justice, the other savages would willingly consent to it, unless the French should be pleased to take as reparation and restitution for the dead some valuable presents of skins, as they are accustomed to do in return for a thing that cannot be restored. They earnestly entreated the French to accept this rather than require the death of the accused which they anticipated would be hard for them to execute, and so doing to forget everything as if it had not occurred.

To this, in accordance with the advice of the holy Fathers, it was decided to reply that the savages should bring and deliver up the two malefactors, in order to ascertain from them their accomplices, and who had incited them to do the deed. This they communicated to La Ferrière for him to report to his companions.

This decision having been made, La Ferrière withdrew to his companions, who upon hearing the decision of the French found this procedure and mode of justice very strange and difficult; since they have no established law among themselves, but only vengeance and restitution by presents. After considering the whole matter and deliberating with one another upon it, they summoned the two murderers and set forth to them the unhappy position into which they had been thrown by the event of this murder, which might cause a perpetual war with the French, from which their women and children would suffer. However much trouble they might give us, and although they might keep us shut up in our settlement and prevent us from hunting, cultivating and tilling the soil, and although we were in too small numbers to keep the river blockaded, as they persuaded themselves to believe in their consultations; still, after all their deliberations, they concluded that it was better to live in peace with the French than in war and perpetual distrust.

Accordingly the savages thus assembled, after finishing their consultation and representing the situation to the accused, asked them if they would not have the courage to go with them to the settlement of the French and appear before them; promising them that they should receive no harm, and assuring them that the French were lenient and disposed to pardon, and would in short go so far in dealing with them as to overlook their offence on condition of their not returning to such evil ways.

The two criminals, finding themselves convicted in conscience, yielded to this proposition and agreed to follow this advice. Accordingly one of them made preparations, arraying himself in such garments and decorations as he could procure, as if he had been invited to go to a marriage or some great festivity. Thus attired, he went to the settlement, accompanied by his father, some of the principal chiefs, and the captain of their company. As to the other murderer, he excused himself from this journey, [208] realizing his guilt of the heinous act and fearing punishment.

When now they had entered the habitation, which was forthwith surrounded by a multitude of the savages of their company, the bridge [209] was drawn up, and all of the French put themselves on guard, arms in hand. They kept a strict watch, sentinels being posted at the necessary points, for fear of what the savages outside might do, since they suspected that it was intended actually to inflict punishment upon the guilty one, who had so freely offered himself to our mercy, and not upon him alone, but upon those also who had accompanied him inside, who likewise were not too sure of their persons, and who, seeing matters in this state, did not expect to get out with their lives. The whole matter was very well managed and carried out, so as to make them realize the magnitude of the crime and have fear for the future. Otherwise there would have been no security with them, and we should have been obliged to live with arms in hand and in perpetual distrust.

After this, the savages suspecting lest something might happen contrary to what they hoped from us, the holy Fathers proceeded to make them an address on the subject of this crime. They set forth to them the friendship which the French had shown them for ten or twelve years back, when we began to know them, during which time we had continually lived in peace and intimacy with them, nay even with such freedom as could hardly be expressed. They added moreover that I had in person assisted them several times in war against their enemies, thereby exposing my life for their welfare; while we were not under any obligations to do so, being impelled only by friendship and good will towards them, and feeling pity at the miseries and persecutions which their enemies caused them to endure and suffer. This is why we were unable to believe, they said, that this murder had been committed without their consent, and especially since they had taken it upon themselves to favor those who committed it.

Speaking to the father of the criminal, they represented to him the enormity of the deed committed by his son, saying that as reparation for it he deserved death, since by our law so wicked a deed did not go unpunished, and that whoever was found guilty and convicted of it deserved to be condemned to death as reparation for so heinous an act; but, as to the other inhabitants of the country, who were not guilty of the crime, they said no one wished them any harm or desired to visit upon them the consequences of it.

All the savages, having clearly heard this, said, as their only excuse, but with all respect, that they had not consented to this act; that they knew very well that these two criminals ought to be put to death, unless we should be disposed to pardon them; that they were well aware of their wickedness, not before but after the commission of the deed; that they had been informed of the death of the two ill-fated men too late to prevent it. Moreover, they said that they had kept it secret, in order to preserve constantly an intimate relationship and confidence with us, and declared that they had administered to the evil-doers severe reprimands, and set forth the calamity which they had not only brought upon themselves, but upon all their tribe, relatives and friends; and they promised that such a calamity should never occur again and begged us to forget this offence, and not visit it with the consequences it deserved, but rather go back to the primary motive which induced the two savages to go there, and have regard for that. Furthermore they said that the culprit had come freely and delivered himself into our hands, not to be punished but to receive mercy from the French.

But the father, turning to the friar, [210] said with tears, there is my son, who committed the supposed crime; he is worthless, but consider that he is a young, foolish, and inconsiderate person, who has committed this act through passion, impelled by vengeance rather than by premeditation: it is in your power to give him life or death; you can do with him what you please, since we are both in your hands.

After this address, the culprit son, presenting himself with assurance, spoke these words. "Fear has not so seized my heart as to prevent my coming to receive death according to my desserts and your law, of which I acknowledge myself guilty." Then he stated to the company the cause of the murder, and the planning and execution of it, just as I have related and here set forth.

After his recital he addressed himself to one of the agents and clerks of the merchants of our Association, named *Beauchaine*, begging him to put him to death without further formality.

Then the holy Fathers spoke, and said to them, that the French were not accustomed to put their fellow-men to death so suddenly, and that it was necessary to have a consultation with all the men of the settlement, and bring forward this affair as the subject of consideration. This being a matter of great consequence, it was decided that it should be carefully conducted and that it was best to postpone it to a more favorable occasion, which would be better adapted to obtain the truth, the present time not being favorable for many reasons.

In the first place, we were weak in numbers in comparison with the savages without and within our settlement, who, resentful and full of vengeance as they are, would have been capable of setting fire on all sides and creating disorder among us. In the second place, there would have been perpetual distrust and no security in our intercourse with them. In the third place, trade would have been injured, and the service of the King impeded.

In view of these and other urgent considerations, it was decided that we ought to be contented with their putting themselves in our power and their willingness to give satisfaction submissively, the father of the criminal on the one hand presenting and offering him to the company, and he, for his part, offering to give up his own life as restitution for his offence, just as his father offered to produce him whenever he might be required.

This it was thought necessary to regard as a sort of honorable amend, and a satisfaction to justice. And it was considered that if we thus pardoned the offence, not only would the criminal receive his life from us, but, also, his father and companions would feel under great obligations. It was thought proper, however, to say to them as an explanation of our action, that, in view of the fact of the criminal's public assurance that all the other savages were in no respect accomplices, or to blame for the act, and had had no knowledge of it before its accomplishment, and in view of the fact that he had freely offered himself to death, it had been decided to restore him to his father, who should remain under obligations to produce him at any time. On these terms and on condition that he should in future render service to the French, his life was spared, that he and all the savages might continue friends and helpers of the French.

Thus it was decided to arrange the matter until the vessels should return from France, when, in accordance with the opinion of the captains and others, a definite and more authoritative settlement was to be concluded. In the mean time we promised them every favor and the preservation of their lives, saying to them, however, for our security, that they should leave some of their children as a kind of hostage, to which they very willingly acceded, and left at the settlement two in the hands of the holy Fathers, who proceeded to teach their letters, and in less than three months taught them the alphabet and how to make the letters.

From this it may be seen that they are capable of instruction and are easily taught, as Father Joseph [211] can testify.

The vessels having safely arrived, Sieur du Pont Gravé, some others, and myself were informed how the affair had taken place, as has been narrated above, when we all decided that it was desirable to make the savages feel the enormity of this murder, but not to execute punishment upon them, for various good reasons hereafter to be mentioned.

As soon as our vessels had entered the harbor of Tadoussac, even on the morning of the next day, [212] Sieur du Pont Gravé and myself set sail again, on a small barque of ten or twelve tons' burden. So also Sieur de la Mothe, together with Father Jean d'Albeau, [213] a friar, and one of the clerks and agent of the merchants, named *Loquin*, embarked on a little shallop, and we set out together from Tadoussac. There remained on the vessel another friar, called Father *Modeste* [214] together with the pilot and master, to take care of her. We arrived at Quebec, the place of our settlement, on the 27th of June following. Here we found Fathers Joseph, Paul, and Pacifique, the friars, [215] and Sieur Hébert [216] with his family, together with the other members of the settlement. They were all well, and delighted at our return in good health like themselves, through the mercy of God.

The same day Sieur du Pont Gravé determined to go to Trois Rivières, where the merchants carried on their trading, and to take with him some merchandise, with the purpose of meeting Sieur des Chesnes, who was already there. He also took with him Loquin, as before mentioned. I stayed at our settlement some days, occupying myself with business relating to it; among other things in building a furnace for making an experiment with certain ashes, directions for which had been given me, and which are in truth of great value; but it requires labor, diligence, watchfulness and skill; and for the working of these ashes a sufficient number of men are needed who are acquainted with this art. This first experiment did not prove successful, and we postponed further trial to a more favorable opportunity.

I visited the cultivated lands, [217] which I found planted with fine grain. The gardens contained all kinds of plants, cabbages, radishes, lettuce, purslain, sorrel, parsley, and other plants, squashes, cucumbers, melons, peas, beans and other vegetables, which were as fine and forward as in France. There were also the vines, which had been transplanted, already well advanced. In a word, you could see everything growing and flourishing. Aside from God, we are not to give the praise for this to the laborers or their skill, for it is probable that not much is due to them, but to the richness and excellence of the soil, which is naturally good and adapted for everything, as experience shows, and might be turned to good account, not only for purposes of tillage and the cultivation of fruit-trees and vines, but also for the nourishment and rearing of cattle and fowl, such as are common in France. But the thing lacking is zeal and affection for the welfare and service of the King.

I tarried some time at Quebec, in expectation of further intelligence, when there arrived a barque from Tadoussac, which had been sent by Sieur du Pont Gravé to get the men and merchandise remaining at that place on the before-mentioned large vessel. Leaving Quebec, I embarked with them for Trois Rivières, where the trading was going on, in order to see the savages and communicate with them, and ascertain what was taking place respecting the assassination above set forth, and what could be done to settle and smooth over the whole matter.

On the 5th of July following I set out from Quebec, together with Sieur de la Mothe, for Trois Rivières, both for engaging in traffic and to see the savages. We arrived, at evening off Sainte Croix, [218] a place on the way so called. Here we saw a shallop coming straight to us, in which were some men from Sieurs du Pont Gravé and des Chesnes, and also some clerks and agents of the merchants. They asked me to despatch at once this shallop to Quebec for some merchandise remaining there, saying that a large number of savages had come for the purpose of making war.

This intelligence was very agreeable to us, and in order to satisfy them, on the morning of the next day I left my barque and went on board a shallop in order to go more speedily to the savages, while the other, which had come from Trois Rivières, continued its course to Quebec. We made such progress by rowing that we arrived at the before-mentioned place on the 7th of July at 3 o'clock in the afternoon. Upon landing, all the savages with whom I had been intimate in their country recognized me. They were awaiting me with impatience, and came up to me very happy and delighted to see me again, one after the other embracing me with demonstrations of great joy, I also receiving them in the same manner. In this agreeable way was spent the evening and remainder of this day, and on the next day the savages held a council among themselves, to ascertain from me whether I would again assist them, as I had done in the past and as I had promised them, in their wars against their enemies, by whom they are cruelly harassed and tortured.

Meanwhile on our part we took counsel together to determine what we should do in the matter of the murder of the two deceased, in order that justice might be done, and that they might be restrained from committing such an offence in future.

In regard to the assistance urgently requested by the savages for making war against their enemies, I replied that my disposition had not changed nor my courage abated, but that what prevented me from assisting them was that on the previous year, when the occasion and opportunity presented, they failed me when the time came; because when they had promised to return with a good number of warriors they did not do so, which caused me to withdraw without accomplishing much. Yet I told them the matter should be taken into consideration, but that for the present it was proper to determine what should be done in regard to the assassination of the two unfortunate men, and that satisfaction must be had. Upon this they left their council in seeming anger and vexation about the matter, offering to kill the criminals, and proceed at once to their execution, if assent were given, and acknowledging freely among themselves the enormity of the affair.

But we would not consent to this, postponing our assistance to another time, requiring them to return to us the next year with a good number of men. I assured them, moreover, that I would entreat the King to favor us with men, means, and supplies to assist them and enable them to enjoy the rest they longed for, and victory over their enemies. At this they were greatly pleased, and thus we separated, after they had held two or three meetings on the subject, costing us several hours of time. Two or three days after my arrival at this place they proceeded to make merry, dance, and celebrate many great banquets in view of the future war in which I was to assist them.

Then I stated to Sieur du Pont Gravé what I thought about this murder; that it was desirable to make a greater demand upon them; that at present the savages would dare not only to do the same thing again but what would be more injurious to us; that I considered them people who were governed by example; that they might accuse the French of being wanting in courage; that if we said no more about the matter they would infer that we were afraid of them: and that if we should let them go so easily they would grow more insolent, bold, and intolerable, and we should even thereby tempt them to undertake greater and more pernicious designs. Moreover I said that the other tribes of savages, who had or should get knowledge of this act, and that it had been unrevenged, or compromised by gifts and presents, as is their custom, would boast that killing a man is no great matter; since the French make so little account of seeing their companions killed by their neighbors, who drink, eat, and associate intimately with them, as may be seen.

But, on the other hand, in consideration of the various circumstances; namely, that the savages do not exercise reason, that they are hard to approach, are easily estranged, and are very ready to take vengeance, that, if we should force them to inflict punishment, there would be no security for those desirous of making explorations among them, we determined to settle this affair in a friendly manner, and pass over quietly what had occurred, leaving them to engage peaceably in their traffic with the clerks and agents of the merchants and others in charge.

Now there was with them a man named *Estienne Brûlé*, one of our interpreters, who had been living with them for eight years, as well to pass his time as to see the country and learn their language and mode of life. He is the one whom I had despatched with orders to go in the direction of the Entouhonorons, [219] to Carantoüan, in order to bring with him five hundred warriors they had promised to send to assist us in the war in which we were engaged against their enemies, a reference to which is made in the narrative of my previous book. [220] I called this man, namely Estienne Brûlé, and asked him why he had not brought the assistance of the five hundred men, and what was the cause of the delay, and why he had not rendered me a report. Thereupon he gave me an account of the matter, a narrative of which it will not be out of place to give, as he is more to be pitied than blamed on account of the misfortunes which he experienced on this commission.

He proceeded to say that, after taking leave of me to go on his journey and execute his commission, he set out with the twelve savages whom I had given him for the purpose of showing the way, and to serve as an escort on account of the dangers which he might have to encounter. They were successful in reaching the place, Carantoüan, but not without exposing themselves to risk, since they had to pass through the territories of their enemies, and, in order to avoid any evil design, pursued a more secure route through thick and impenetrable forests, wood and brush, marshy bogs, frightful and unfrequented places and wastes, all to avoid danger and a meeting with their enemies.

But, in spite of this great care, Brûlé and his savage companions, while crossing a plain, encountered some hostile savages, who were returning to their village and who were surprised and worsted by our savages, four of the enemy being killed on the spot and two taken prisoners, whom Brûlé and his companions took to Carantoüan, by the inhabitants of which place they were received with great affection, a cordial welcome, and good cheer, with the dances and banquets with which they are accustomed to entertain and honor strangers.

Some days were spent in this friendly reception; and, after Brûlé had told them his mission and explained to them the occasion of his journey, the savages of the place assembled in council to deliberate and resolve in regard to sending the five hundred warriors asked for by Brûlé.

When the council was ended and it was decided to send the men, orders were given to collect, prepare, and arm them, so as to go and join us where we were encamped before the fort and village of our enemies. This was only three short days' journey from Carantoüan, which was provided with more than eight hundred warriors, and strongly fortified, after the manner of those before described, which have high and strong palisades well bound and joined together, the quarters being constructed in a similar fashion.

After it had been resolved by the inhabitants of Carantoüan to send the five hundred men, these were very long in getting ready, although urged by Brûlé, to make haste, who explained to them that if they delayed any longer they would not find us there. And in fact they did not succeed in arriving until two days after our departure from that place, which we were forced to abandon, since we were too weak and worn by the inclemency of the weather. This caused Brûlé, and the five hundred men whom he brought, to withdraw and return to their village of Carantoüan. After their return Brûlé was obliged to stay, and spend the rest of the autumn and all the winter, for lack of company and escort home. While awaiting, he busied himself in exploring the country and visiting the tribes and territories adjacent to that place, and in making a tour along a river [221] that debouches in the direction of Florida, where are many powerful and warlike nations, carrying on wars against each other. The climate there is very temperate, and there are great numbers of animals and abundance of small game. But to traverse and reach these regions requires patience, on account of the difficulties involved in passing the extensive wastes.

He continued his course along the river as far as the sea, [222] and to islands and lands near them, which are inhabited by various tribes and large numbers of savages, who are well disposed and love the French above all other nations. But those who know the Dutch [223] complain severely of them, since they treat them very roughly. Among other things he observed that the winter was very temperate, that it snowed very rarely, and that when it did the snow was not a foot deep and melted immediately.

After traversing the country and observing what was noteworthy, he returned to the village of Carantoüan, in order to find an escort for returning to our settlement. After some stay at Carantoüan, five or six of the savages decided to make the journey with Brûlé. On the way they encountered a large number of their enemies, who charged upon Brûlé and his companions so violently that they caused them to break up and separate from each other, so that they were unable to rally: and Brûlé, who had kept apart in the hope of escaping, became so detached from the others that he could not return, nor find a road or sign in order to effect his retreat in any direction whatever. Thus he continued to wander through forest and wood for several days without eating, and almost despairing of his life from the pressure of hunger. At last he came upon a little footpath, which he determined to follow wherever it might lead, whether toward the enemy or not, preferring to expose himself to their hands trusting in God rather than to die alone and in this wretched manner. Besides he knew how to speak their language, which he thought might afford him some assistance.

But he had not gone a long distance when he discovered three savages loaded with fish repairing to their village. He ran after them, and, as he approached, shouted at them, as is their custom. At this they turned about, and filled with fear were about to leave their burden and flee. But Brûlé speaking to them reassured them, when they laid down their bows and arrows in sign of peace, Brûlé on his part laying down his arms. Moreover he was weak and feeble, not having eaten for three or four days. On coming up to them, after he had told them of his misfortune and the miserable condition to which he had been reduced, they smoked together, as they are accustomed to do with one another and their acquaintances when they visit each other. They had pity and compassion for him, offering him every assistance, and conducting him to their village, where they entertained him and gave him something to eat.

But as soon as the people of the place were informed that an *Adoresetoüy* had arrived, for thus they call the French, the name signifying *men of iron*, they came in a rush and in great numbers to see Brûlé. They took him to the cabin of one of the principal chiefs, where he was interrogated, and asked who he was, whence he came, what circumstance had driven and led him to this place, how he had lost his way, and whether he did not belong to the French nation that made war upon them. To this he replied that he belonged to a better nation, that was desirous solely of their acquaintance and friendship. Yet they would not believe this, but threw themselves upon him, tore out his nails with their teeth, burnt him with glowing firebrands, and tore out his beard, hair by hair, though contrary to the will of the chief.

During this fit of passion one of the savages observed an *Agnus Dei*, which he had attached to his neck, and asked what it was that he had thus attached to his neck, and was on the point of seizing it and pulling it off. But Brûlé said to him, with resolute words, If you take it and put me to death, you will find that immediately after you will suddenly die, and all those of your house. He paid no attention however to this, but continuing in his malicious purpose tried to seize the *Agnus Dei* and tear it from him, all of them together being desirous of putting him to death, but previously of making him suffer great pain and torture, such as they generally practise upon their enemies.

But God, showing him mercy, was pleased not to allow it, but in his providence caused the heavens to change suddenly from the serene and fair state they were in to darkness, and to become filled with great and thick clouds, upon which followed thunders and lightnings so violent and long continued that it was something strange and awful. This storm caused the savages such terror, it being not only unusual but unlike anything they had ever heard, that their attention was diverted and they forgot the evil purpose they had towards Brûlé, their prisoner. They accordingly left him without even unbinding him, as they did not dare to approach him. This gave the sufferer an opportunity to use gentle words, and he appealed to them and remonstrated with them on the harm they were doing him without cause, and set forth to them how our God was enraged at them for having so abused him.

The captain then approached Brûlé, unbound him, and took him to his house, where he took care of him and treated his wounds. After this there were no dances, banquets, or merry-makings to which Brûlé was not invited.

So after remaining some time with these savages, he determined to proceed towards our settlement.

Taking leave of them, he promised to restore them to harmony with the French and their enemies, and cause them to swear friendship with each other, to which end he said he would return to them as soon as he could. Thence he went to the country and village of the Atinouaentans, [224] where I had already been; the savages at his departure having conducted him for a distance of four days' journey from their village. Here Brûlé remained some time, when, resuming his journey towards us he came by way of the *Mer Douce*, [225] boating along its northern shores for some ten days, where I had also gone when on my way to the war.

And if Brûlé had gone further on to explore these regions, as I had directed him to do, it would not have been a mere rumor that they were preparing war with one another. But this undertaking was reserved to another time, which he promised me to continue and accomplish in a short period with God's grace, and to conduct me there that I might obtain fuller and more particular knowledge.

After he had made this recital, I gave him assurance that his services would be recognized, and encouraged him to continue his good purpose until our return, when we should have more abundant means to do that with which he would be satisfied. This is now the entire narrative and recital of his journey from the time he left me [226] to engage in the above-mentioned explorations; and it afforded me pleasure in the prospect thereby presented me of being better able to continue and promote them.

With this purpose he took leave of me to return to the savages, an intimate acquaintance with whom had been acquired by him in his journeys and explorations. I begged him to continue with them until the next year, when I would return with a good number of men, both to reward him for his labors, and to assist as in the past the savages, his friends, in their wars.

Resuming the thread of my former discourse, I must note that in my last and preceding voyages and explorations I had passed through numerous and diverse tribes of savages not known to the French nor to those of our settlement, with whom I had made alliances and sworn friendship, on condition that they should come and trade with us, and that I should assist them in their wars; for it must be understood that there is not a single tribe living in peace, excepting the Nation Neutre. According to their promise, there came from the various tribes of savages recently discovered some trade in peltry, others to see the French and ascertain what kind of treatment and welcome would be shown them. This encouraged everybody, the French on the one hand to show them cordiality and welcome, for they honored them with some attentions and presents, which the agents of the merchants gave to gratify them; on the other hand, it encouraged the savages, who promised all the French to come and live in future in friendship with them, all of them declaring that they would deport themselves with such affection towards us that we should have occasion to commend them, while we in like manner were to assist them to the extent of our power in their wars.

The trading having been concluded, and the savages having taken their leave and departed, we left Trois Rivières on the 14th of July of this year. The next day we arrived at our quarters at Quebec, where the barques were unloaded of the merchandise which had remained over from the traffic and which was put in the warehouse of the merchants at that place.

Now Sieur de Pont Gravé went to Tadoussac with the barques in order to load them and carry to the habitation the provisions necessary to support those who were to remain and winter there, and I determined while the barques were thus engaged to continue there for some days in order to have the necessary fortifications and repairs made.

At my departure from the settlement I took leave of the holy Fathers, Sieur de la Mothe, and all the others who were to stay there, giving them to expect that I would return, God assisting, with a good number of families to people the country. I embarked on the 26th of July, together with the Fathers Paul and Pacifique, [227] the latter having wintered here once and the other having been here a year and a half, who were to make a report of what they had seen in the country and of what could be done there. We set out on the day above mentioned from the settlement for Tadoussac, where we were to embark for France. We arrived the next day and found our vessels ready to set sail. We embarked, and left Tadoussac for France on the 13th of the month of July, 1618, and arrived at Honfleur on the 28th day of August, the wind having been favorable, and all being in good spirits.

ENDNOTES:

201. Champlain made a voyage to New France in 1617, but appears to have kept no journal of its events. He simply observes that nothing occurred worthy of remark. *Vide* issue of 1632, Quebec ed.,

p. 969. Sagard gives a brief narrative of the events that occurred that year. Vol. I. pp. 34-44.

202. Eustache Boullé. His father was Nicolas Boullé, Secretary of the King's Chamber, and his mother was Marguerite Alix. *Vide* Vol. I. p. 205 *et passim.*

203. Nicolas de La Mothe, or de la Motte le Vilin. He had been Lieutenant of Saussaye in 1613, when Capt. Argall captured the French colony at Mount Desert. *Vide Les Voyages de Champlain,* 1632, Quebec ed., p. 773; *Relation de la Nouvelle France,* Père Biard, p. 64.

204. *Fauquets.* Probably the common Tern, or Sea Swallow. *Sterna hirundo.* Peter Kalm, on his voyage in 1749, says "Terns, *sterna hirundo, Linn,* though of a somewhat darker colour than the common ones, we found after the forty-first degree of north latitude and forty-seventh degree of west longitude from *London,* very plentifully, and sometimes in flocks of some hundreds; sometimes they settled, as if tired, on our ship." *Kalm's Travels,* 1770, Vol. I. p. 23.

205. St. John's day was June 24th.

206. According to Sagard they were assassinated about the middle of April, 1617. *Hist. Canada,* Vol. I. p. 42.

207. Sagard says the French, on account of this affair, were menaced by eight hundred savages of different nations who were assembled at Trois Rivières. *Vide Histoire du Canada,* 1636, Vol. I. p.42. The statement, "on estoit menacé de huict cens Sauvages de diuerse nations, qui festoient assemblez és Trois Rivieres à dessein de venir surprendre les François & leur coupper à tous la gorge, pour preuenir la vengeance qu'ils eussent pû prendre de deux de leurs hommes tuez par les Montagnais environ la my Auril de l'an 1617," is, we think, too strong. The savages were excited and frightened by the demands of the French, who desired to produce upon their minds a strong moral impression, in order to prevent a recurrence of the murder, which was a private thing, in which the great body of the savages had no part. They could not be said to be hostile, though they prudently put themselves in a state of defence, as, under the circumstances, it was very natural they should do.

208. They were then at Trois Rivières.

209. The moat around the habitation at Quebec was fifteen feet wide and six feet deep, constructed with a drawbridge to be taken up in case of need. *Vide* Vol II p. 182.

210. Probably Père le Caron, who was in charge of the mission at Quebec at that time.

211. *Vide Histoire du Canada*, par Sagard, 1636, Vol. I. p 45.

212. They arrived on St. John's day, *antea, note 205*, and consequently this was the 2tth of June, 1618.

213. Jean d'Olbeau.

214. Frère Modeste Guines. *Vide Histoire du Canada*, par Sagard, à Paris, 1636, Vol. I.p. 40.

215. Joseph le Caron, Paul Huet, and Pacifique du Plessis.

216. Louis Hébert, an apothecary, settled at Port Royal in La Cadie or Nova Scotia, under Poutrincourt, was there when, in 1613, possession was taken in the name of Madame de Guercheville. He afterward took up his abode at Quebec with his family, probably in the year 1617. His eldest daughter Anne was married at Quebec to Estienne Jonquest, a Norman, which was the first marriage that took place with the ceremonies of the Church in Canada. His daughter Guillemette married William Couillard, and to her Champlain committed the two Indian girls, whom he was not permitted by Kirke to take with him to France, when Quebec was captured by the English in 1629. Louis Hébert died at Quebec on the 25th of January, 1627. *Histoire du Canada*, Vol. I. pp. 41, 591.

217. These fields were doubtless those of Louis Hébert, who was the first that came into the country with his family to live by the cultivation of the soil.

218. Platon. *Vide* Vol. 1., note 155.

219. Champlain says, *donné charge d'aller vers les Entouhonorons à Carantouan*. By reference to the map of 1632. it will be seen that the Entouhonorons were situated on the southern borders of Lake Ontario. They are understood by Champlain to be a part at least of the Iroquois; but the Carantouanais, allies of the Hurons, were south of them, occupying apparently the upper waters of the Susquehanna. A dotted line will be seen on the same map, evidently intended to

mark the course of Brûlé's journey. From the meagre knowledge which Champlain possessed of the region, the line can hardly be supposed to be very accurate, which may account for Champlain's indefinite expression as cited at the beginning of this note.

> The Entouhonorons, Quentouoronons, Tsonnontouans, or Senecas constituted the most western and most numerous canton of the Five Nations. *Vide Continuation of the New Discovery,* by Louis Hennepin, 1699, p. 95; also Origin of the name Seneca in Mr. O. H. Marshall's brochure on *De la Salle among the Senecas,* pp. 43-45.

220. *Vide antea,* p. 124.

221. The River Susquehanna.

222. He appears to have gone as far south at least as the upper waters of
Chesapeake Bay.

223. The Dutch fur-traders. *Vide History of the State of New York* by John
Romeyn Brodhead, Vol. I. p. 44 *et passim.*

224. Attigonantans or Attignaouantans the principal tribe of the Hurons,
sometimes called *Les bons Iroquis,* as they and the Iroquois were of
the same original stock. *Vide* Vol. I. p. 276, note 212.

225. Lake Huron. For the different names which have been attached to this
lake, *vide Local Names of Niagara Frontier,* by Orsamus H. Marshall,
1881, P. 37.

226. Brûlé was despatched on his mission Sept 8, 1615. *Vide antea,* p. 124.

As we have already stated in a previous note, it was the policy of Champlain to place competent young men with the different tribes of savages to obtain that kind of information which could only come from an actual and prolonged residence with them. This enabled him to secure not only the most accurate knowledge of their domestic habits and customs, the character and spirit of their life, but these young men by their long residence with the savages acquired a good knowledge of their language, and were able to act as interpreters. This was a matter of very great importance, as it was often necessary for Champlain to communicate with the different tribes in making treaties of friendship, in discussing questions of war with their enemies, in settling disagreements among themselves, and in making arrangements with them for the yearly purchase of their peltry. It was not easy to obtain suitable persons for this important office. Those who had the intellectual qualifications, and who had any high aspirations, would not naturally incline to pass years in the stupid and degrading associations, to say nothing of the hardships and deprivations, of savage life. They were generally therefore adventurers, whose honesty and fidelity had no better foundation than their selfish interests. Of this sort was this Étienne Brûlé, as well as Nicholas Marsolet and Pierre Raye, all of whom turned traitors, selling themselves to the English when Quebec was taken in 1629. Of Brûlé, Champlain uses the following emphatic language: "Lé truchement Bruslé à qui l'on donnoit cent pistolles par an, pour inciter les sauuages à venir à la traitte, ce qui estoit de tres-mauuais exemple, d'enuoyer ainsi des personnes si maluiuans, que l'on eust deub chastier seuerement, car l'on recognoissoit cet homme pour estre fort vicieux, & adonné aux femmes; mais que ne fait faire l'esperance du gain, qui passe par dessus toutes considerations." *Vide issue of* 1632, Quebec ed., pp. 1065, 1229.

But among Champlain's interpreters there were doubtless some who bore a very different character. Jean Nicolet was certainly a marked exception. Although Champlain does not mention him by name, he appears to have been in New France as early as 1618, where he spent many years among the Algonquins, and was the first Frenchman who penetrated the distant Northwest. He married into one of the most respectable families of Quebec, and is often mentioned in the Relations des Jésuites. *Vide* a brief notice of him in *Discovery and Exploration of the Mississippi Valley,* by John Gilmary Shea, 1852, p. xx. A full account of his career has recently been published, entitled *History of the Discovery of the Northwest by John Nicolet in* 1634, *with a Sketch of his Life.* By C. W. Butterfield. Cincinnati, 1881. *Vide* also *Détails fur la Vie de Jean Nicollet,* an extract from *Relation des Jésuites,* 1643, in *Découveries,* etc, par Pierre Margry, p. 49.

227. Paul Huet and Pacifique du Plessis. The latter had been in New France more than a year and a half, having arrived in 1615. *Vide antea,* pp. 104-5.

EXPLANATION OF TWO GEOGRAPHICAL MAPS OF NEW FRANCE.

It has seemed to me well to make some statements in explanation of the two geographical maps. Although one corresponds to the other so far as the harbors, bays, capes, promontories, and rivers extending into the interior are concerned, nevertheless they are different in respect to the bearings.

The smallest is in its true meridian, in accordance with the directions of Sieur de Castelfranc in his book on the mecometry of the magnetic needle [228] where I have noted, as will be seen on the map, several declinations, which have been of much service to me, so also all the altitudes, latitudes, and longitudes, from the forty-first degree of latitude to the fifty-first, in the direction of the North Pole, which are the confines of Canada, or the Great Bay, where more especially the Basques and Spaniards engage in the whale fishery. In certain places in the great river St. Lawrence, in latitude 45°, I have observed the declination of the magnetic needle, and found it as high as twenty-one degrees, which is the greatest I have seen.

The small map will serve very well for purposes of navigation, provided the needle be applied properly to the rose [229] indicating the points of the compass. For instance, in using it, when one is on the Grand Bank where fresh fishing is carried on, it is necessary, for the sake of greater convenience, to take a rose where the thirty-two points are marked equally, and put the point of the magnetic needle 12, 15, or 16 degrees from the *fleur de lis* on the northwest side, which is nearly a point and a half, that is north a point northwest or a little more, from the fleur de lis of said rose, and then adjust the rose to the compass. By this means the latitudes of all the capes, harbors, and rivers can be accurately ascertained.

I am aware that there are many who will not make use of it, but will prefer to run according to the large one, since it is made according to the compass of France, where the magnetic needle varies to the northeast, for the reason that they are so accustomed to this method that it is difficult for them to change. For this reason I have prepared the large map in this manner, for the assistance of the majority of the pilots and mariners in the waters of New France, fearing that if I had not done so, they would have ascribed to me a mistake, not knowing whence it proceeded. For the small plans or charts of Newfoundland are, for the most part, different in all their statements with respect to the positions of the lands and their latitudes. And those who may have some small copies, reasonably good, esteem them so valuable that they do not communicate a knowledge of them to their country, which might derive profit therefrom.

Now the construction of these maps is such that they have their meridian in a direction north-northeast, making west west-northwest, which is contrary to the true meridian of this place, namely, to call north-northeast north, for the needle instead of varying to the northwest, as it should, varies to the northeast as if it were in France. The consequence of this is that error has resulted, and will continue to do so, since this antiquated custom is practised, which they still retain, although they fall into grave mistakes.

They also make use of a compass marked north and south; that is, so that the point of the magnetic needle is directly on the *fleur de lis*. In accordance with such a compass many construct their small maps, which seems to me the better way, and so approach nearer to the true meridian of New France, than the compasses of France proper, which point to the northeast. It has come about, consequently, in this way that the first navigators who sailed to New France thought there was no greater deviation in going to these parts than to the Azores, or other places near France, where the deviation is almost imperceptible in navigation, the navigators having the compasses of France, which point northeast and represent the true meridian. In sailing constantly westward with the purpose of reaching a certain latitude, they laid their course directly west by their compass, supposing that they were sailing on the one parallel where they wished to go. By thus going constantly in a straight line and not in a circle, as all the parallels on the surface of the globe run, they found after having traversed a long distance, and as they were approaching the land, that they were some three, four, or five degrees farther south than they ought to be, thus being deceived in their true latitude and reckoning.

It is true, indeed, that, when the weather was fair and the fun clearly visible, they corrected their latitude, but not without wondering how it happened that their course was wrong, which arose in consequence of their sailing in a straight instead of a circular line according to the parallel, so that in changing their meridian they changed with regard to the points of the compass, and consequently their course. It is, They therefore, very necessary to know the meridian, and the declination of the magnetic needle, for this knowledge can serve all navigators. This is especially so in the north and south, where there are greater variations in the magnetic needle, and where the meridians of longitude are smaller, so that the error, if the declination were not known, would be greater. This abovementioned error has accordingly arisen, because navigators have either not cared to correct it, or did not know how to do so, and have left it in the state in which it now is. It is consequently difficult to abandon this manner of sailing in the regions of New France.

This has led me to make this large map, not only that it might be more minute than the small one, but also in order to satisfy navigators, who will thus be able to sail as they do according to their small maps; and they will excuse me for not making it better and more in detail, for the life of a man is not long enough to observe things so exactly that at least something would not be found to have been omitted. Hence inquiring and pains-taking persons will, in sailing, observe things not to be found on this map, but which they add to it, so that in the courte of time there will be no doubt as to any of the localities indicated. At least it seems to me that I have done my duty, so far as I could, not having sailed to put on my map anything that I have seen, and thus giving to the public special knowledge of what had never been described, nor so carefully explored as I have done it. Although in the past others have written of these things, yet very little in comparison with what we have explored within the past ten years.

MODE OF DETERMINING A MERIDIAN LINE.

Take a small piece of board, perfectly level, and place in the middle a needle C, three inches high, so that it shall be exactly perpendicular. Expose it to the sun before noon, at 8 or 9 o'clock, and mark the point B at the end of the shadow cast by the needle. Then opening the compasses, with one point on C and the other on the shadow B, describe an arc AB. Leave the whole in this position until afternoon when you see the shadow just reaching the arc at A. Then divide equally the arc AB, and taking a rule, and placing it on the points C and D, draw a line running the whole length of the board, which is not to be moved until the observation is completed. This line will be the meridian of the place you are in.

And in order to ascertain the declination of the place where you are with reference to the meridian, place a compass, which must be rectangular, along the meridian line, as shown in the figure above, there being upon the card a circle divided into 360 degrees. Divide the circle by two diametrical lines; one representing the north and south, as indicated by EF, the other the east and west, as indicated by GH. Then observe the magnetic needle turning on its pivot upon the card, and you will see how much it deviates from the fixed meridian line upon the card, and how many degrees it varies to the northeast of northwest.

CHAMPLAIN'S LARGE MAP.

GEOGRAPHICAL CHART OF NEW FRANCE, MADE BY SIEUR DE CHAMPLAIN OF SAINTONGE, CAPTAIN IN ORDINARY FOR THE KING IN THE MARINE. MADE IN THE YEAR 1612.

I have made this map for the greater convenience of the majority of those who navigate on these coasts, since they sail to that country according to compasses arranged for the hemisphere of Asia. And if I had made it like the small one, the majority would not have been able to use it, owing to their not knowing the declinations of the needle. [230]

Observe that on the present map north-northeast stands for north, and west-northwest for west; according to which one is to be guided in ascertaining the elevation of the degrees of latitude, as if these points were actually east and west, north and south, since the map is constructed according to the compasses of France, which vary to the northeast. [231]

SOME DECLINATIONS OF THE MAGNETIC NEEDLE, WHICH I HAVE CAREFULLY OBSERVED.

Cap Breton . . . . . . 14° 50'
Cap de la Have . . . . 16° 15'
Baye Ste Mane . . . . 17° 16'
Port Royal . . . . . . 17° 8'
En la grande R. St Laurent 21°

St Croix . . . . 17° 32'
Rivière de Norumbegue. 18° 40'
Quinibequi . . . . . . 19° 12'
Mallebarre . . . . . . 18° 40'

All observed by Sieur de Champlain, 1612.

REFERENCES ON CHAMPLAIN'S LARGE MAP.

A. Port Fortuné.
B. Baye Blanche.
C. Baye aux Isles.
D. Cap des Isles.
E. Port aux Isles.
F. Isle Haute.
G. Isle des Monts Déserts.
H. Cap Corneille.
I. Isles aux Oiseaux.
K. Cap des Deux Bayes.
L. Port aux Mines
M. Cap Fourchu.
N. Cap Nègre.
O. Port du Rossignol.
P. St. Laurent.
Q. Rivière de l'Isle Verte.
R. Baye Saine.
S. Rivière Sainte Marguerite
T. Port Sainte Hélène.
V. Isle des Martires.
X. Isles Rangées.
Y. Port de Savalette.
Z. Passage du Glas.

1. Port aux Anglois. 2. Baye Courante. 3. Cap de Poutrincourt. 4. Isle Gravée. 5. Passage Courant. 6. Baye de Gennes. 7. Isle Perdue. 8. Cap des Mines. 9. Port aux Coquilles. 10. Isles Jumelles. 11. Cap Saint Jean. 12. Isle la Nef. 13. La Heronniére Isle. 14. Isles Rangées. 15. Baye Saint Luc. 16. Passage du Gas. 17. Côte de Montmorency. 18. Rivière de Champlain. 19. Rivière Sainte Marie. 20. Isle d'Orléans. 21. Isle de Bacchus.

NOTE—The reader will observe that in a few instances the references are wanting on the map.

CHAMPLAIN'S NOTE TO THE SMALL MAP.

On the small map [232] is added the strait above Labrador between the fifty-third and sixty-third degrees of latitude, which the English have discovered during the present year 1612, in their voyage to find, if possible, a passage to China by way of the north. [233] They wintered at a place indicated by this mark, 6. But it was not without enduring severe cold, and they were obliged to return to England, leaving their leader in the northern regions. Within fix months three other vessels have set out, to penetrate, if possible, still farther, and, at the same time, to search for the men who were left in that region.

GEOGRAPHICAL MAP OF NEW FRANCE, IN ITS TRUE MERIDIAN.

Made by Sieur Champlain, Captain for the King in the Marine. 1613.

+o Matou-ouescariny. [Note: This figure is inverted on the map. *Vide antea*, note 59, p. 62.]

o+ Gaspay.

oo Ouescariny. [Note: *Vide antea*, note 47, pp. 59, 81. The figure oo is misplaced and should be where o-o is on the map, on the extreme western border near the forty-seventh degree of north latitude.]

o-o Quenongebin. [Note: This figure o-o on the map occupies the place which should be occupied by oo. *Vide antea*, p. 58, note 46.]

A. Tadoussac.

B. Lesquemain.

C. Isle Percée.

D. Baye de Chaleur.

E. Isles aux Gros Yeux. [Note: A cluster of islands of which the Island of Birds is one.]

H. Baye Françoise.

I. Isles aux Oyseaux.

L. Rivière des Etechemins. [Note: This letter, placed between the River
St. John and the St. Croix, refers to the latter.]
M. Menane.
N. Port Royal.
P. Isle Longue.
Q. Cap Fourchu.
R. Port au Mouton.
S. Port du Rossignol. [Note: The letter S appears twice on the coast of
La Cadie. The one here referred to is the more westerly.]
SS. Lac de Medicis. [Note: This reference is probably to the Lake of Two
Mountains, which will be seen on the map west of Montreal.]
T. Sesambre.
V. Cap des Deux Bayes.
3. L'Isle aux Coudres.
4. Saincte Croix. [Note: St. Croix on the map is where a cross surmounted
by the figure 4 may be seen.]
4. Rivière des Etechemins. [Note: This appears to refer to the Chaudière. *Vide* vol. I. p. 296.]
5. Sault. [Note: This refers to the Falls of Montmorency.]
6. Lac Sainct Pierre.
7. Rivière des Yroquois.
9. Isle aux Lieures.
10. Rivière Platte. [Note: A small river flowing into Mal Bay. *Vide* Vol. I. p. 295; also *Les Voyages de Champlain*, Quebec ed., p. 1099.]
11. Mantane. [Note: *Vide* Vol. I. p 234.]
40. Cap Saincte Marie. [Note: The figures are wanting. Cape St. Mary is on
the southern coast of Newfoundland. *Vide* Vol I. p. 232.]

ENDNOTES:

228. The determination of longitudes has from the beginning been environed with almost insuperable difficulties. At one period the declination of the magnetic needle was supposed to furnish the means of a practical solution. Sebastian Cabot devoted considerable attention to the subject, as did likewise Peter Plancius at a later date. Champlain appears to have fixed the longitudes on his smaller map by calculations based on the variation of the needle, guided by the principles laid down by Guillaume de Nautonier, Sieur de Castelfranc, to whose work he refers in the text. It was entitled, *Mécométrie de l'eymant c'est à dire la manière de mesurer les longitudes par le moyen de l'eymant.* This rare volume is not to be found as far as my inquiries extend, in any of the incorporated libraries on this continent. There is however a copy in the Bodleian Library at Oxford, to which in the catalogue is given the bibliographical note: *Six livres. Folio. Tolose, 1603.*

> It is hardly necessary to add that the forces governing the variation of the needle, both local and general, are so inconstant that the hope of fixing longitudes by it was long since abandoned.
>
> The reason for the introduction of the explanation of the maps at this place will be seen *antea,* p. 39.

229. The rose is the face or card of the mariner's compass. It was anciently called the fly. Card may perhaps be derived from the Italian cardo, a thistle, which the face of the compass may be supposed to resemble. On the complete circle of the compass there are thirty-two lines drawn from the centre to the circumference to indicate the direction of the wind. Each quarter of the circle, or 90°, contains eight lines representing the points of the compass in that quarter. They are named with reference to the cardinal points from which they begin, as: 1, north, 2, north by east, 3, north-northeast; 4, northeast by north; 5, northeast; 6, northeast by east; 7, east- northeast; 8, east by north. The points in each quarter are named in a similar manner.

230. The above title is on the large map of 1612. This note is on the upper left-hand corner of the same map.

231. For this note see the upper right-hand corner of the map.

232. In Champlain's issue in 1613, the note here given was placed in the preliminary matter to that volume. It was placed there probably after the rest of the work had gone to press. We have placed it here in connection with other matter relating to the maps, where it seems more properly to belong.

233. This refers to the fourth voyage of Henry Hudson, made in 1610, for the purpose here indicated. He penetrated Lomley's Inlet, hoping to find a passage through to the Pacific Ocean, or, as it was then called, the South Sea, and thus find a direct and shorter course to China. He passed the winter at about 52° north latitude, in that expanse of water which has ever since been appropriately known ass Hudson's Bay. A mutiny having broken out among his crew, he and eight others having been forced into a small boat, on the 21st of June, 1611, were set adrift on the sea, and were never heard of afterward.

A part of the mutinous crew arrived with the ship in England, and were immediately thrown into prison. The following year, 1612, an expedition under Sir Thomas Button was sent out to seek for Hudson, and to prosecute the search still further for a northwest passage It is needless to add that the search was unsuccessful.

A chart by Hudson fortunately escaped destruction by the mutineers. Singularly enough, an engraving of it, entitled, TABVLA NAVTICA, was published by Heffel Gerritz at Amsterdam the same year. Champlain incorporated the part of it illustrating Hudson's discovery in his smaller map, which is dated the fame year, 1612. He does not introduce it into his large map, although that is dated likewise 1612. A facsimile of the Tabula Nautica is given in Henry Hudson the Navigator, by G. M. Asher, LL.D. published by the Hakluyt Society in 1860.